BRAZILIAN RHYTHMS
COORDINATION STUDIES

READING, SYSTEMS AND CHALLENGES

ISBN - 978-85-924528-1-0

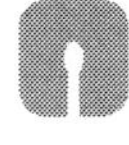 I dedicate this book to my dear teacher **Lilian Carmona**, for her instruction and the momentum which sparked this study of rhythmic independence.

INDEX

ABOUT THE AUTHOR

Ramon Motagner began his musical studies at 12, becoming a professional soon thereafter, and has been playing different genres ever since. From 1992 to 2006 he played tours and recordings with singer/songwriter **Johnny Alf**. In 1998, he joins drummer **Alexandre Cunha** for the video **"Brazilian Duet – Ultrapassando Limites"** *(Exceeding Limits)*.

His first solo album, **Boyya** (Mix House) was released in 2000 and features **Hermeto Paschoal, Mané Silveira, Sizão Machado**, among others. Together with bassist Gilberto de Syllos, in 2003, the book **"Bateria e Contrabaixo na Música Brasileira"** (Drums and Bass in Brazilian Music) is released through publishing company Editora Lumiar, and recently relaunched by Editora Irmãos Vitale. Also played as sideman in numerous TV shows as a hired musician by SBT TV station.

In 2006 the second album **"SAMBASÓ"** is released, and in that same year, the DVD **"Vassourinhas na Música Brasileira"** (Brushes in Brazilian Music), the first dvd/class made in Brazil about the subject.

In 2012 comes the third solo album, **"Atemporal"** (Timeless) through DG Productions,

In 2006 Ramon begins playing with singer **Luiza Possi** in recordings and shows. As well, with singer **Virgínia Rosa**.

Member of the octet **São Paulo Ska Jazz**, and in March 2017 joins the band **Falamansa**.

Took part in **9Beats Drum Summer Camp** in China in 2017, alongside great drummers from around the world, and is currently promoting his fourth album **"Moldura dos Pés"** (Feet Frame).

Holds a Bachelor's Degree in Popular music from FITO in Osasco, São Paulo.

FOREWORD

This method is fruit of the extensive use and experimentation of my own material with students for over a decade. It seeks to help Brazilian music students develop the aptitude for the execution of rhythms, however, ascending some steps further in the sense of rhythmic independence.

In a general way, I was inspired by the systems methodology proposed by **Gary Chester**'s book *"The New Breed – Systems for the Development of Your Own Creativity"*, which was previously used by **Alan Dawson**, reproduced and published by **John Ramsay** in the book *"The Drummer's Complete Vocabulary As Taught by Alan Dawson"*. I also used concepts of two other books I'd studied widely: *"4-Way Coordination"*, by **Marvin Dahlgren** and **Elliot Fine**, and a series of reading content pertaining to *"The Complete Book of Modern Drumming"*, by **Norman Grossman**.

With these ideas in mind I created systems and rhythmic interpretation when reading two or three-voice reading. Prior to this, I'd concentrated on the concept of harmonic coordination, proposing systems where some voices overlap.

The result of this mix – and of years of experimenting with students – shaped the necessity of exposing this to other drum students who are interested in projecting themselves further than coordination practice.

HOW TO USE THIS BOOK

The book fundamentally pursues the development of rhythmic coordination. It aims to generate interdependence among limbs and thus, after continuous practice, produce a new richer approach to phrasing when playing Brazilian rhythms. This can be executed more freely, with the liberty to create new rhythmic elements and by adding varations, and it could instigate one's own language, or, at least, some personal intentions. These requisites are currently lacking, in a world full of excessive information yet at a loss when it comes to concentration and focus.

I created reading content with this mindset, with gradual increasing difficulty, and these you should practice by applying to the systems proposed. The systems are first exposed as variations for **Samba**, followed by more of these for genres **Baião, Frevo, Maracatu, Ijexá**, finalizing with a few **additional systems**.

Next, I proposed systems and preparatory exercises for **two-voice reading**, then **three-voice reading** following respectively. At the end, I presented some systems and reading in **5/4** to play the genre **Jequibau**, and systems and reading in **7/8** for **Samba** and **Baião**.

Lastly, I suggest exercises for Harmonic Independence in Brazilian rhythms.

I find it necessary to emphasize to all students (not only those who struggle to read music) that they should practice initially each note combination using 4/4 time separately, as shown on **page 9** of this book. This will provide confidence and firmness while practicing.

Since the necessary speed and fluency as well as future applications will arise through constant practice, try to study at a slow tempo and focus on coordination. Do not discard the metronome from your routine for it is fundamental in your development as a professional drummer; precision is needed, as is the complete control over aspects that concern tempo, so as to use them in your favor.

No different from other instruments, playing the drums requires a good dose of patience and determination for development. As a psychomotor activity, it relies on movement repetition for full, or at least high level proficiency.

Restating the cliché: *practice makes perfect*, and this applies perfectly to drum practice.

With this study content, I believe students who are truly interested and persistent will expand and reach a new degree of excellence in performance, at which point one's particular language is pursued.

If you are left-handed, think of the proposed systems yet inverted, and if this is halfway true, find the most advantageous path.

Our journey requires time and determination.

Shall we?

KEY

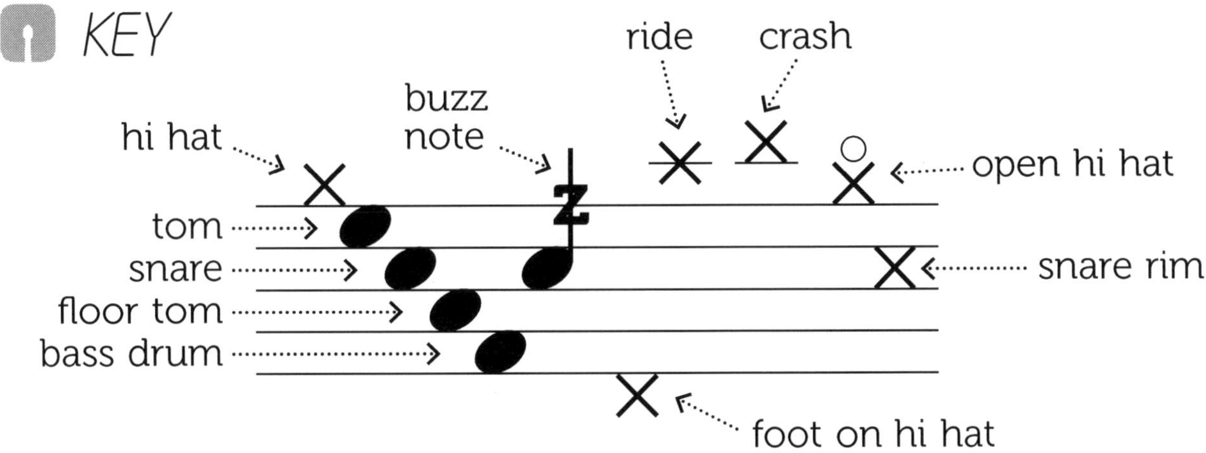

NOTE COMBINATIONS

Examples: how to study the systems initially applying the figures above:

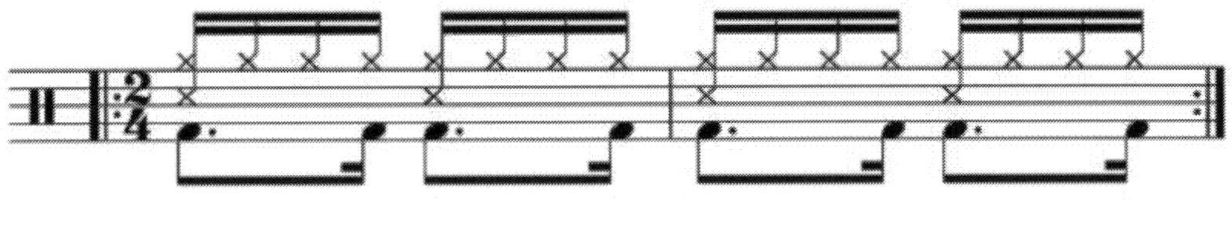

In the examples above, applying **combination 1** to **System 1** for **Samba (pg. 14)**, and in the second, applying **combination 12** to **System 13** for **Samba (pg.15)**.

 CODE NOTATION FOR SYSTEMS

left hand   right hand

left foot   right foot

 snare rim

 bass drum

 ride

 hi hat

 floor tom

 snare drum

EXAMPLES

  READ RIGHT HAND » SNARE

  READ RIGHT FOOT » BASS DRUM

   READ RIGHT HAND » RIDE / FLOOR TOM

  READ LEFT HAND, LEFT AND RIGHT FOOT

UNIT I

 SYSTEMS AND READING

Practice by reading and systems aims to expand rhythmic possibilities, being that it generates unusual coordinations, which extends far beyond grooves with few variations.

You should practice these systems while maintaining the proposed rhythmic paths. Further, apply the reading (pg. 29) that follows below the systems to all suggested rhythms.

As previously explained, before reading all through, concentrate and repeat system by system several times, with each rhythmic combination that will be used in this book. These are the quaternary note groups and their variations.

After this initial study separating figures, begin the reading and, if you make a mistake, return to the beginning of the bar where it happened and try to read as fluidly as possible. **With time and persistence, you will become able to fully read each section perfectly.**

The systems used in this unit allow for separate readings, with the right and left hand, as well as the right and left foot.

> **REMEMBER TO FIND
> THE BEST WAY
> TO PRACTICE IF
> YOU ARE NOT
> RIGHT-HANDED.**

SAMBA

audio reference

CIDADE VAZIA
MILTON BANANA TRIO
CD BALANÇANDO

Samba originated from old hand drum beats brought by Africans that came as slaves to Brazil. Under the influence of genres **Jongo** and **Lundu**, these beats were usually associated with religious elements and also created a certain communication ritual through music and dance, involving percussion and body movement.

It is the most representative and widely recognized genre of popular Brazilian music, which, naturally considering a country with continental dimensions, grew countless ramifications and sub-genres. To name a few: **Samba de Roda, Samba Funk, Partido Alto, Samba Choro, Pagode, Bossa Nova** and **Samba Jazz**. Samba itself, like other many other Afro-Brazilian and Afro-Cuban rhythms, was created using percussion instruments, and its adaptation for drumset ocurred in the beginning of the 20th century.

The book will explore aspects from the viewpoint of rhythmic coordination and its applicability, and is more focused on **Samba Jazz**, which is played somewhat more loosely, especially in Brazilian capitals such as São Paulo, Rio de Janeiro, Belo Horizonte (Minas Gerais), and Brasília.

I used various examples of **tamborim** rhythms, a two-bar pattern popularly known in Brazil as **"Telecoteco"** and its inversion, meaning that you play the second bar first. There are different standpoints on the matter, so I adopted this nomenclature abdicating from anthropological and historiographical aspects.

Photo: Fernando Maia | RioTur

TELECOTECO

or

Here is a basic Samba groove already adapted for drumset, from which we will develop our systems:

$\bullet$ = 85 bpm

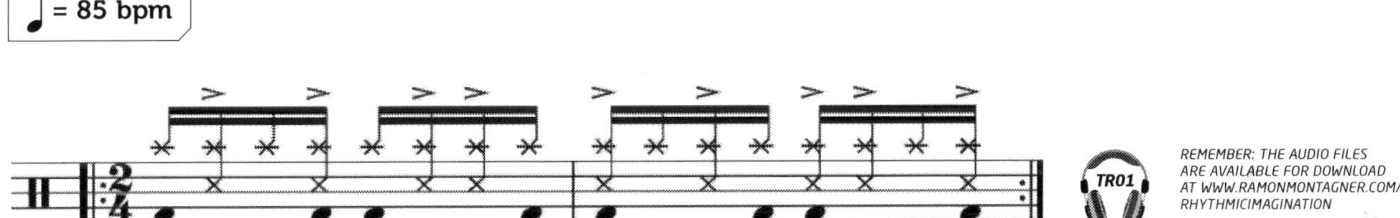

or

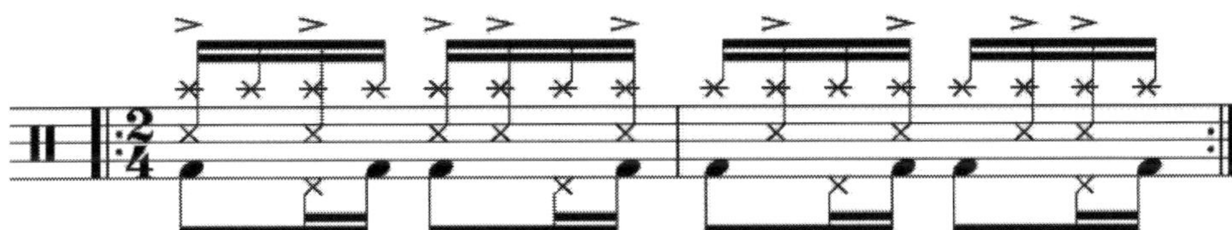

COORDINATION SYSTEMS FOR SAMBA

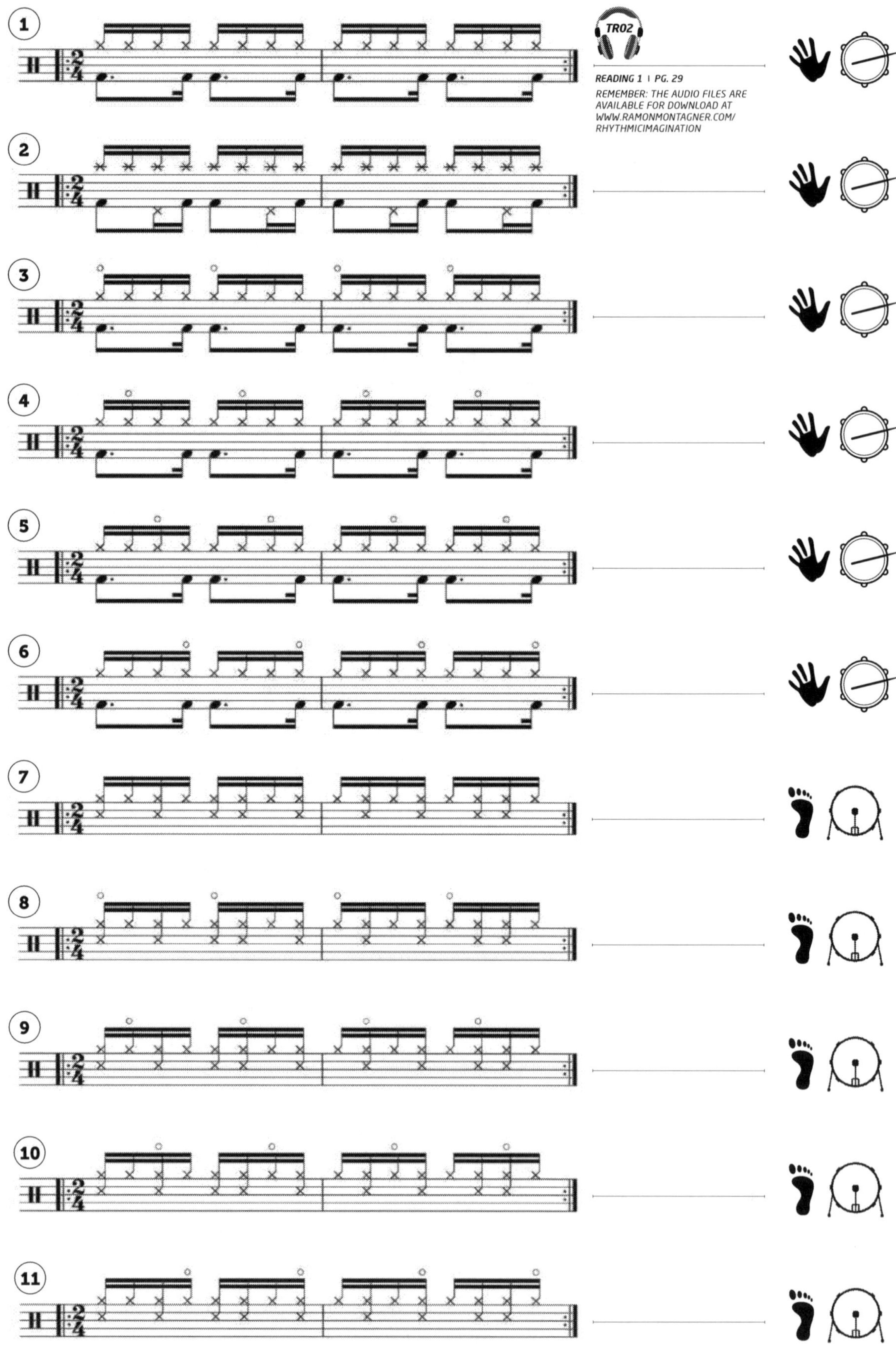

TR03
READING 3 | PG. 31

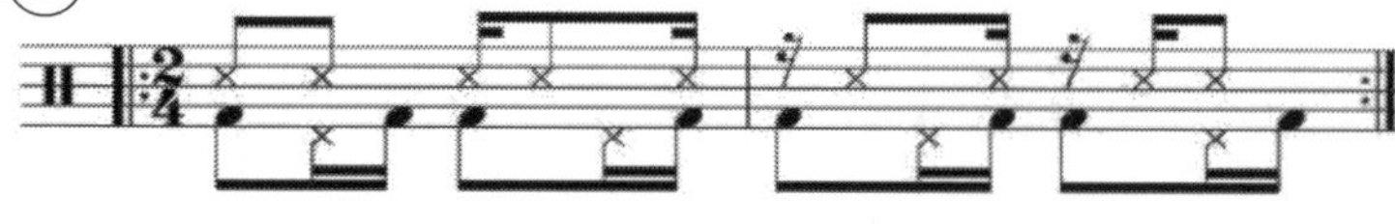

TR04

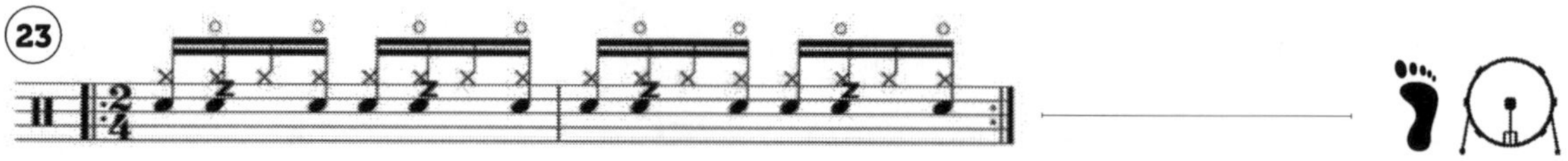

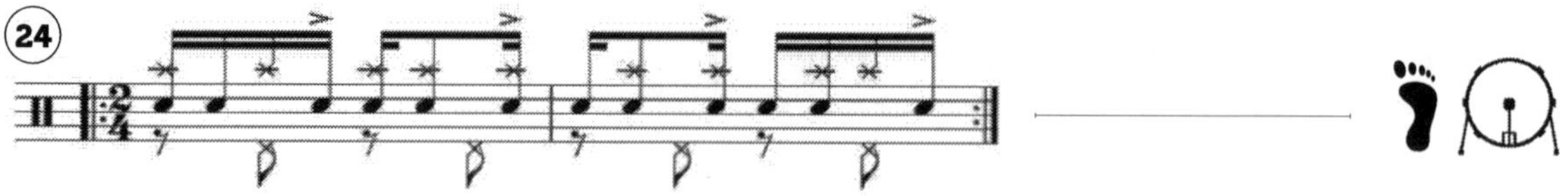

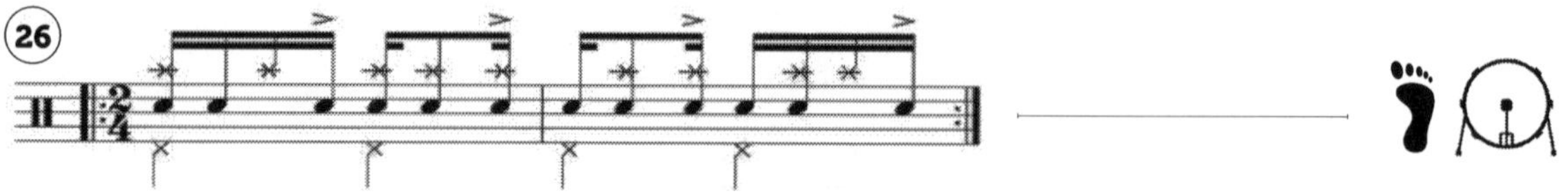

READING 5 | PG. 33

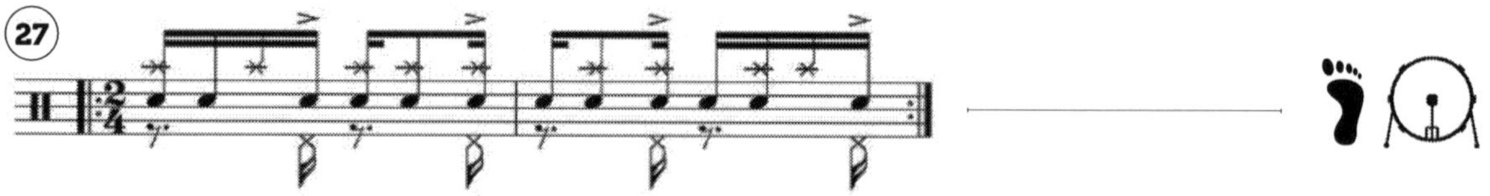

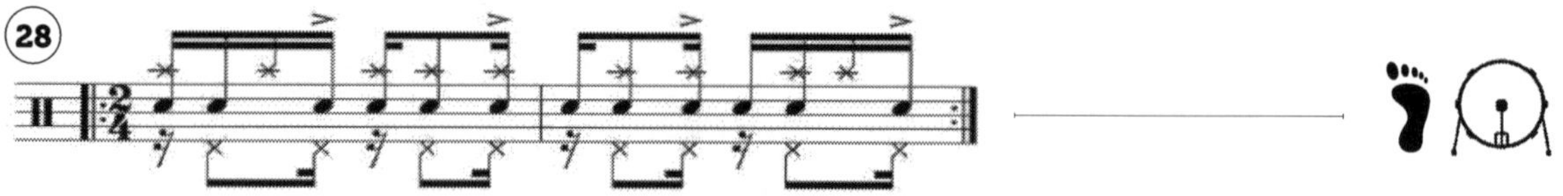

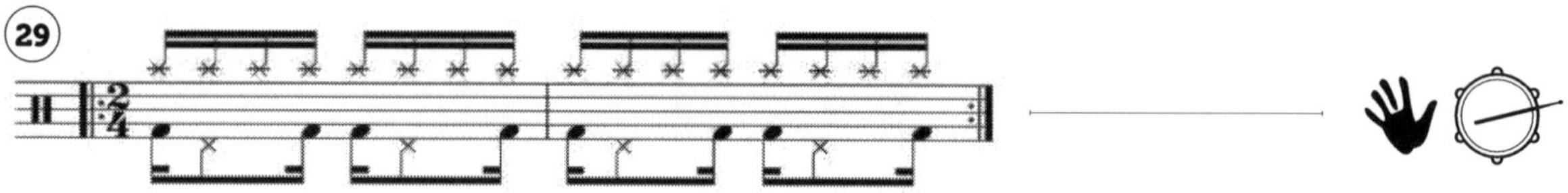

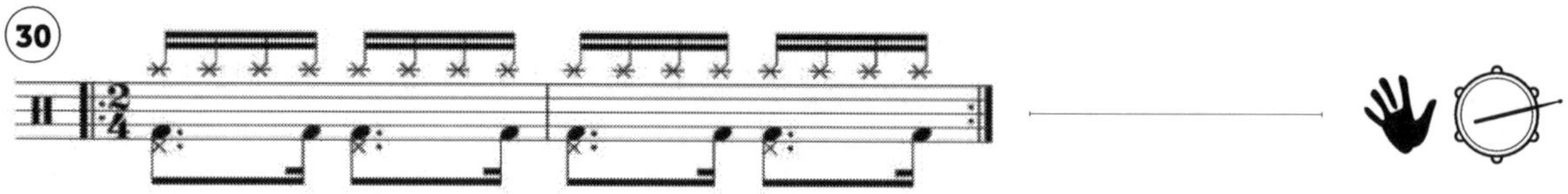

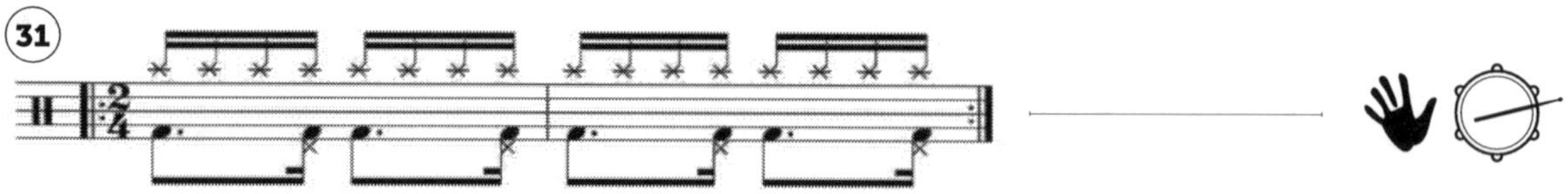

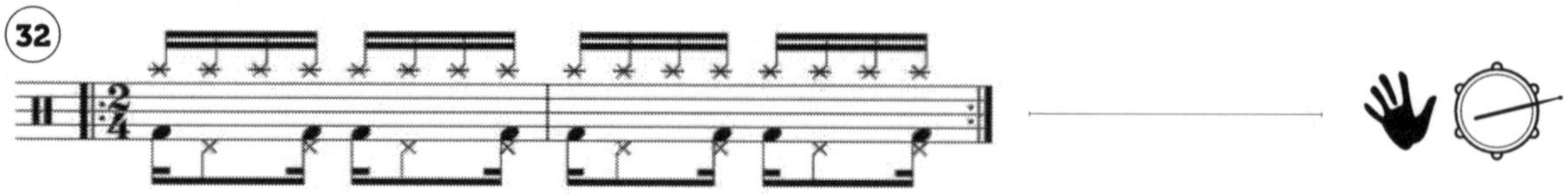

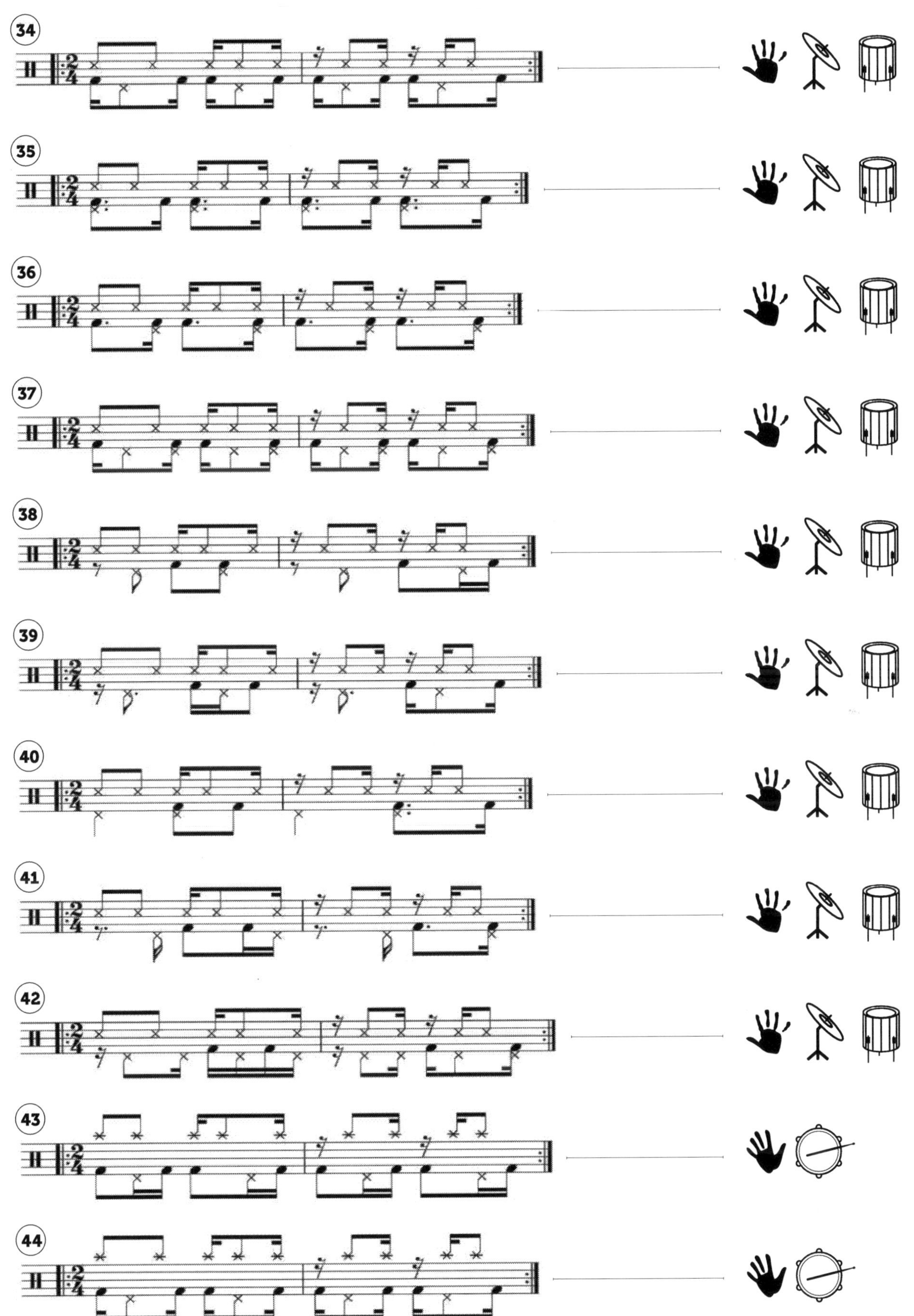

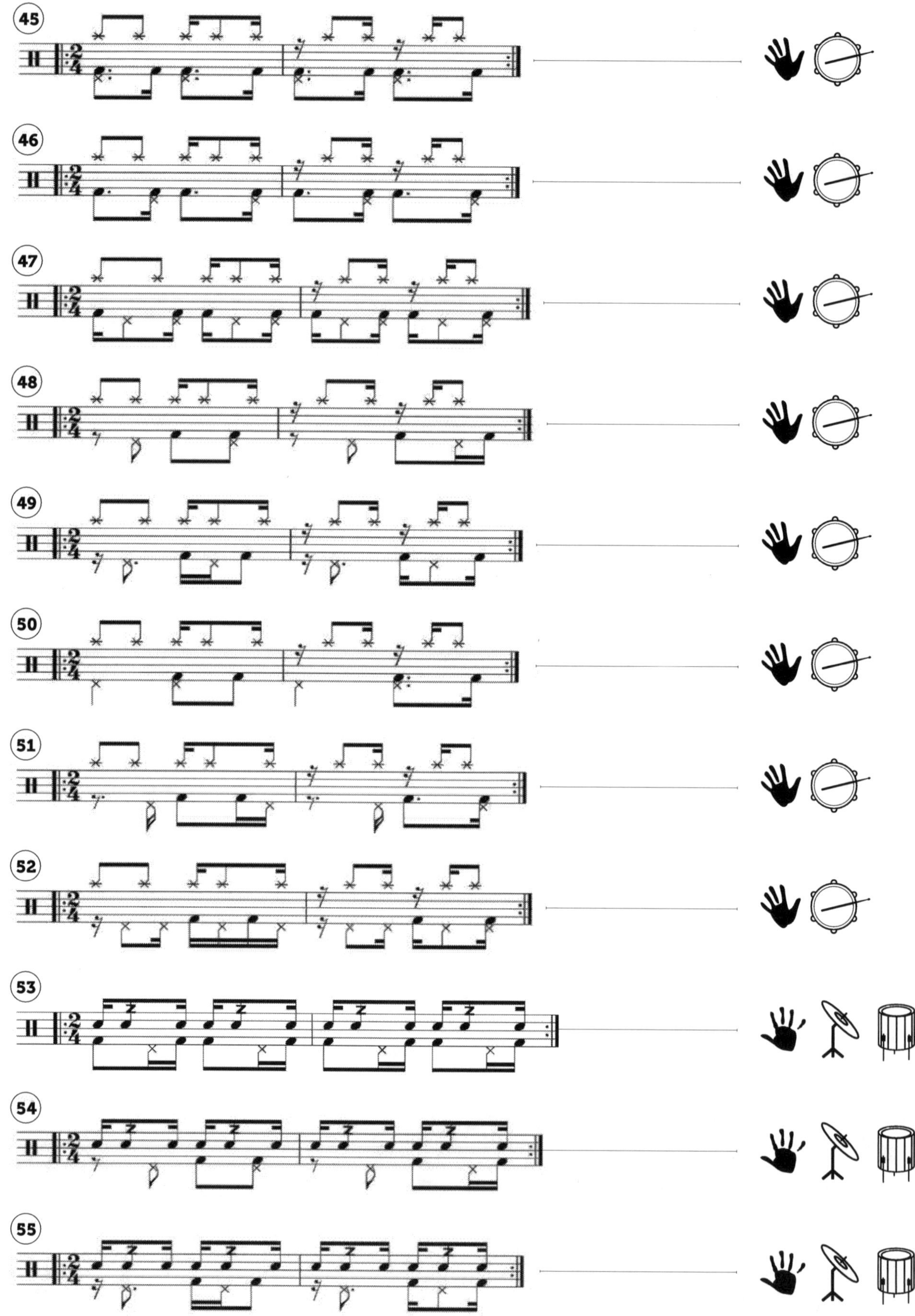

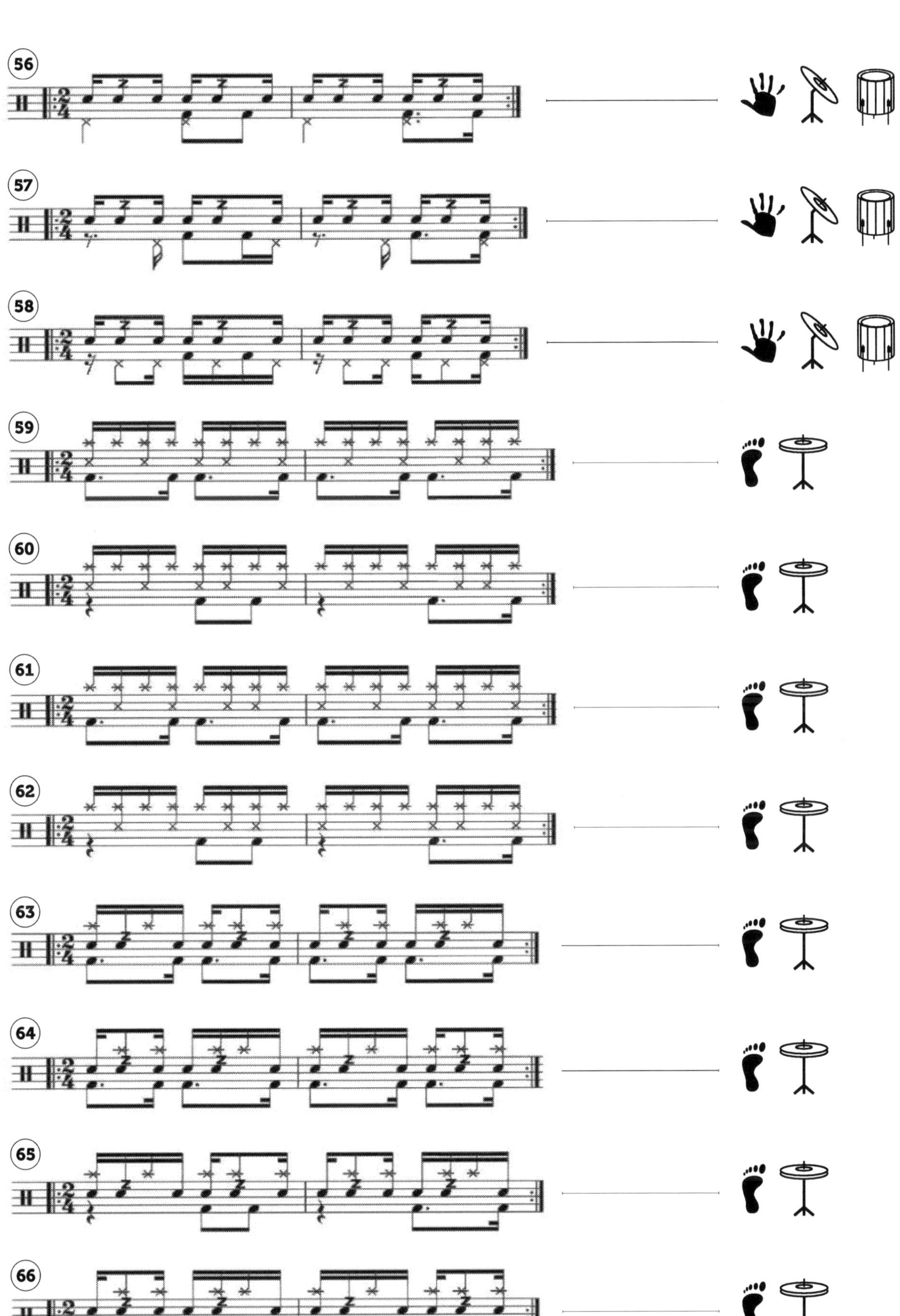

BAIÃO

One of the music and dance genres that is played the most in northeast Brazil, just like Samba, Baião also used percussion instruments like **zabumba** and **triangle**, and later adapted for drumset. The **accordion** gives it harmonic and melodic support.

Its origin lies in a synthesis of African elements from **Lundu** culture and Portuguese music existant in Brazil at the end of the 18th century. Baião produces a very syncopated style and is originally based on the urban day-to-day, full of lust and humor, turning it into a festive dance style.

Luiz Gonzaga, or "Gonzagão", is perhaps its greatest patron, and the expansion and consolidation in Brazil's music scene began in the 1940s.

Baião also has ramifications and variations from sub-genres **Xaxado, Xote** and **Rastapé**, or **Quadrilha**.

Below are the basic grooves already adapted for drumset, from which we will develop our systems:

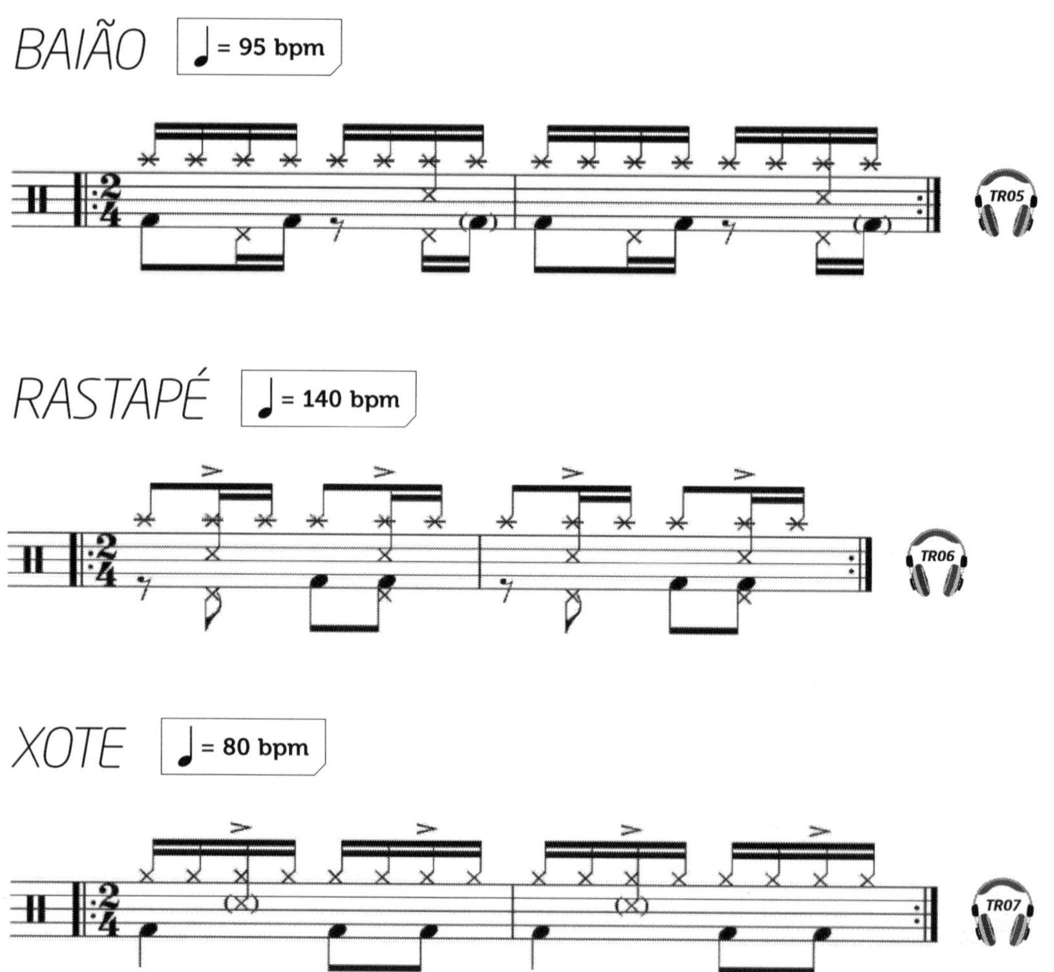

Systems 1 to 13 are more directed towards **Baião** and **Xaxado**, and **systems 14 and 15** towards **Xote** and **Rastapé**, respectively.

COORDINATION SYSTEMS FOR BAIÃO

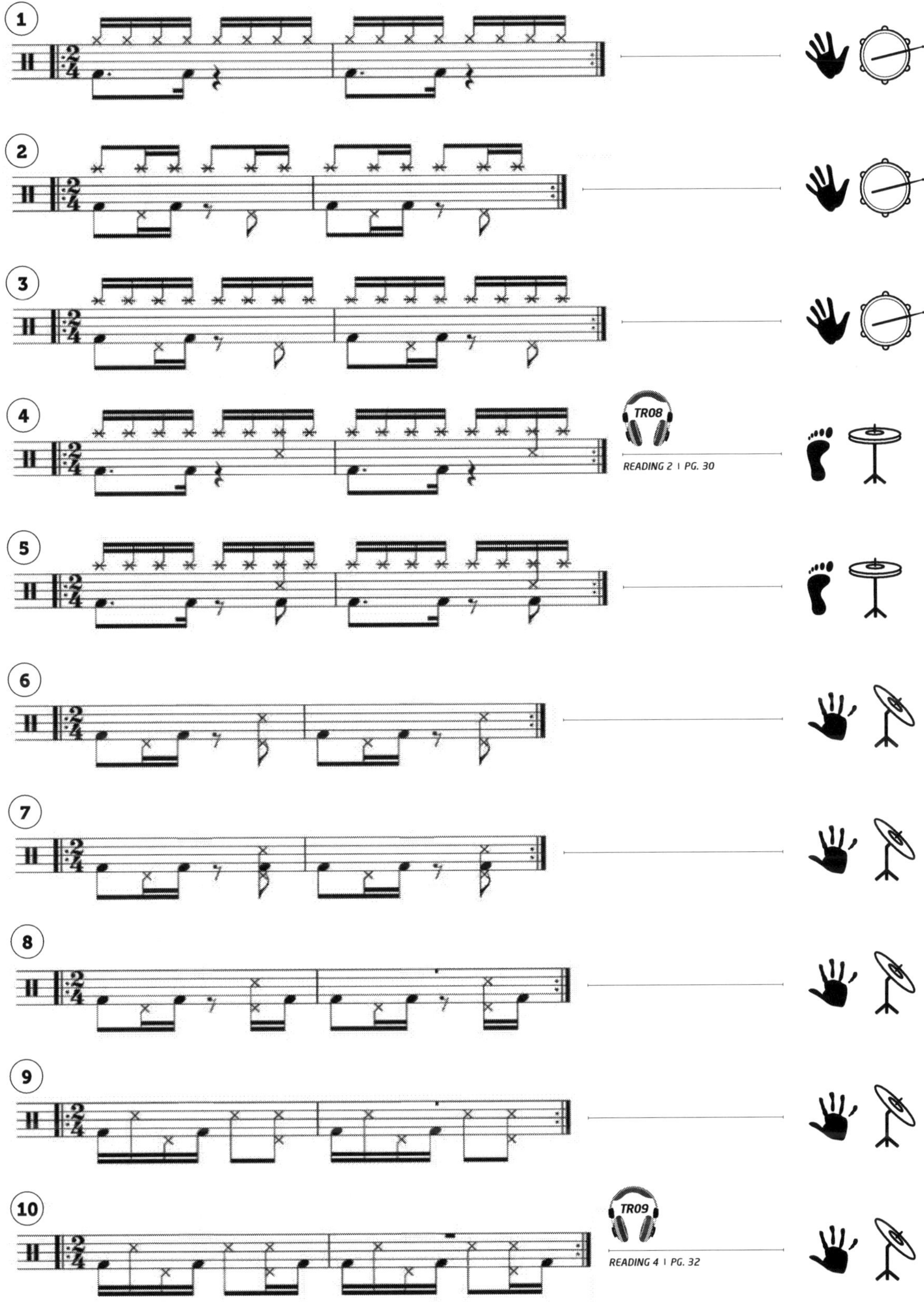

11

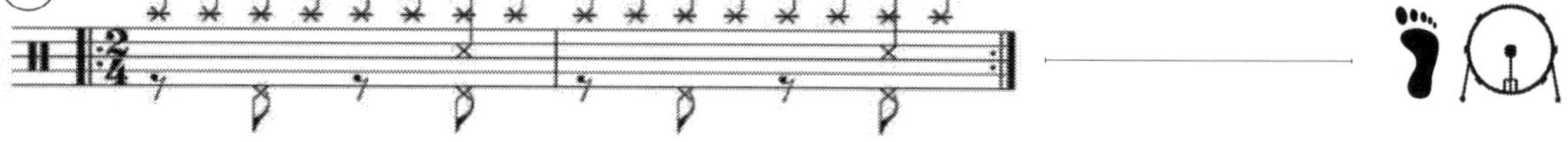

12

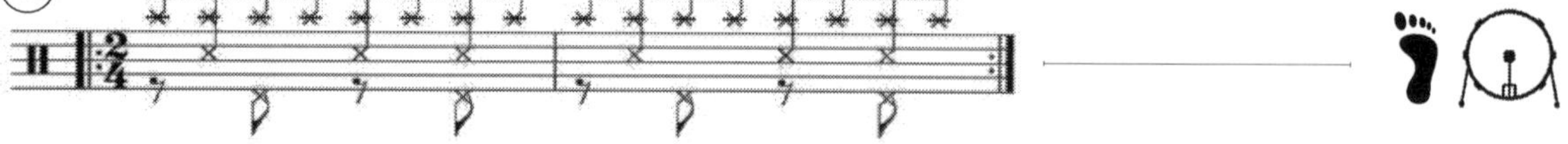

13

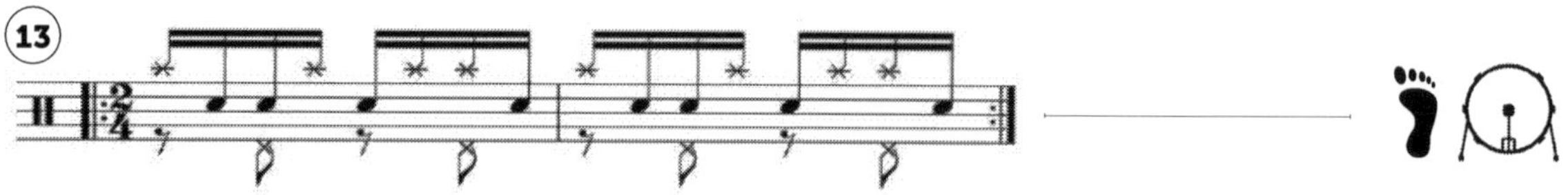

14

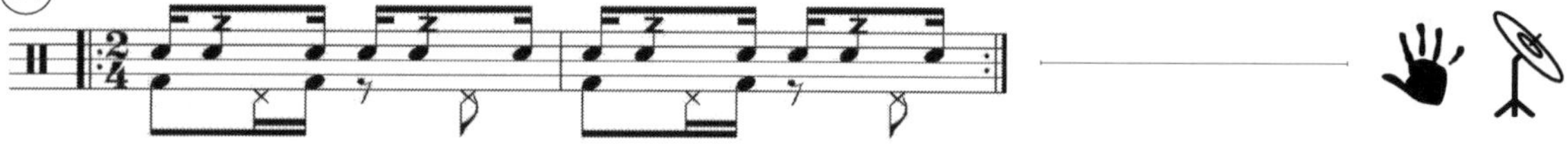

RASTAPÉ

15

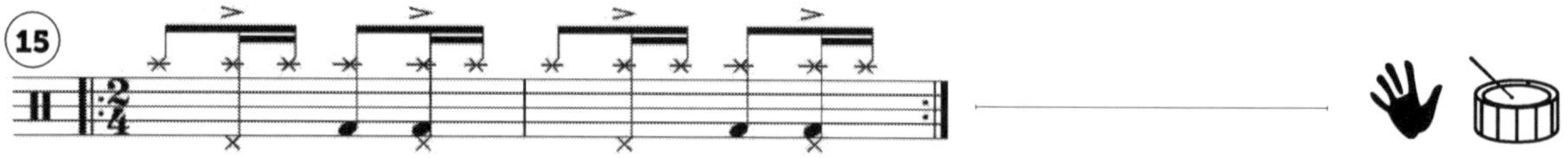

XOTE

16

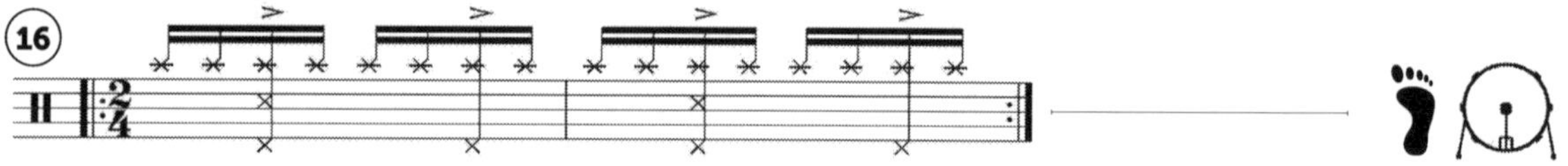

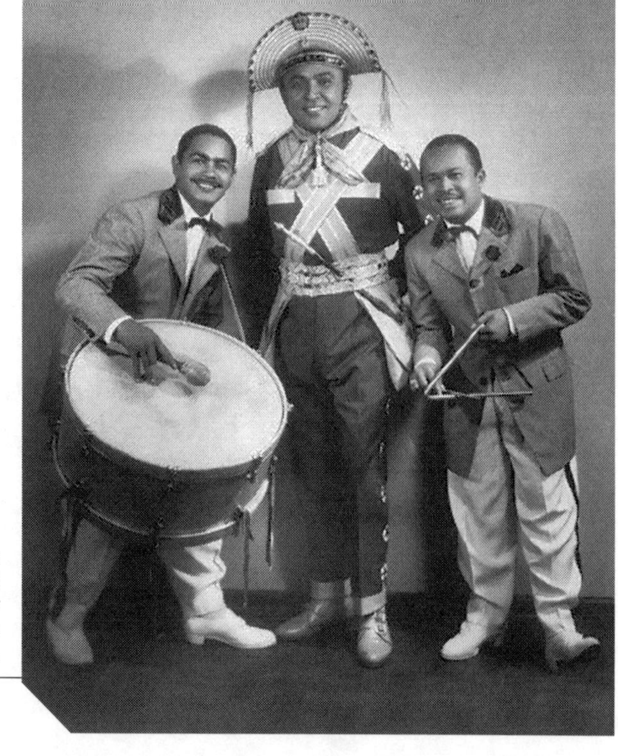

In the middle, Luiz Gonzaga, or "Gonzagão", accompanied by musicians holding a zabumba and a triangle.

FREVO

Originally from Pernambuco, northeast Brazil, this music and dance genre was highly influenced by **Maxixes, Polcas** and **Dobrados** ("Doubled") played by military bands during Carnaval around the end of the 19th century.

It is a hot and fast rhythm, often used today during Carnaval in Brazil. The word **Frevo** comes from fervor, and in this context became: *"Efervescence, agitation, confusion, fuss; tight crowd of popular masses coming and going in opposite directions as is Carnaval"*, according to the book **"Vocabulário Pernambucano"** by **Pereira da Costa**.

There are innumerable variations such as: **Frevo de Bloco, Frevo Canção** and **Frevo de Rua**, an exclusively instrumental genre. This one possesses

Arrastão do Frevo Recife (city). Photo: André Nery | PCR

three sub-modalities, **Frevo Coqueiro** (coconut tree), which takes its name from the very high notes played by brass instruments constantly standing out; **Frevo Ventania** (gust), due to its very fast phrasing by the saxophones, and **Frevo Abafo** (muffle), which is played when one group walks toward the other. At that moment, both groups play as loud as possible, prioritizing volume over technique, looking to "muffle" the other's music; among others. However, we will stick to the basic groove generally played by blocos (street groups) and bands like **Spok Frevo Orquestra**, from great drummers **Augusto Silva** and (maestro) **Adelson Silva**.

Systems 1 and 3 below are based on the classic frevo groove already adapted for drumset, leading with the **snare drum**, and **system 2** is based on an adaptation of the traditional frevo **snare groove** but using the ride cymbal, making it sound more jazz-like. See a basic frevo groove on drums, that is where we will draw the following systems from:

REMEMBER: THE AUDIO FILES ARE AVAILABLE FOR DOWNLOAD AT WWW.RAMONMONTAGNER.COM/ RHYTHMICIMAGINATION

COORDINATION SYSTEMS FOR FREVO

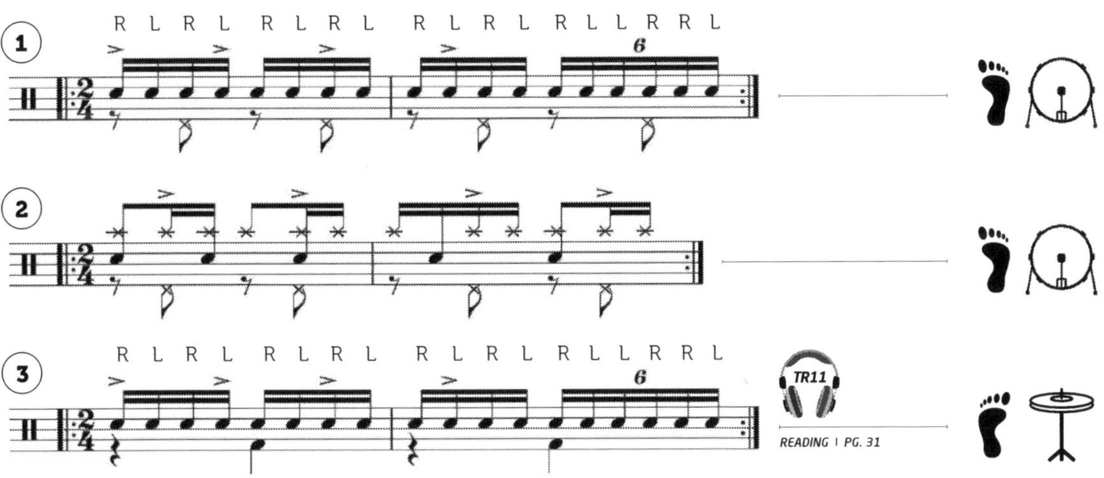

MARACATU

Maracatu is a manifestation of popular Brazilian culture mixed with its African heritage. It probably emerged between the 17th and 18th century, where the state of Pernambuco is found today, specifically in cities like Recife and Olinda.

Like most popular manifestations in the country, it is a mix of Native American, African and European cultures and used percussion instruments like the alfaia – large heavy drum with leather heads and rope tuning – as well as **snare drums, gonguês** (percussion bells) and **caxixis** (percussion shakers). **Maestro Guerra Peixe** was one of the pioneers of **Maracatu** arrangements for orchestras and wrote the important book **"Maracatus do Recife"**, where he systematized and promoted the rhythm in the academic arena.

Traditional Maracatu groups are called **Nações** (Nations) and parade the streets during Carnaval in Recife, northeast Brazil.

The following systems contain varied grooves from different "baques". In the **first two**, you will read with the **bass drum**, and **the others, right hand on the ride or floor tom**. See a basic **Maracatu** groove already adapted for the drumset. It is a **Maracatu de Baque Virado**, from which I created the following systems:

Maracatu Nação Encanto da Alegria Recife PE
Photo: Clélio Tomaz | PCR

COORDINATION SYSTEMS FOR MARACATU

Maracatu Nação Encanto da Alegria
Photo Clélio Tomaz | PCR

Ijexá originally comes from Nigéria, Africa, and arrived in Brazil with slaves from the colonial period. It is the music of religious rituals, with tranquil steady rhythm, and is also part of street processions initiated by those adept to this religion.

It is the rhythm that weaves **Afoxés**, groups that put on this Afro-Brazilian cultural manifestation, so present in Carnavals that take place in northeast Brazil. In the beginning, only percussion instruments such as **agogo bells** and **atabaques** (hand drums) were used. Also, it is very common in the repertoire of renowned Brazilian artists.

Perhaps the most widely known group that plays **Ijexá** in Brazil is **"Afoxé Filhos de Gandhi"**.

This is a basic **Ijexá** groove adapted for drumset and often heard in original music by **Gilberto Gil** and **Djavan**:

REMEMBER: THE AUDIO FILES ARE AVAILABLE FOR DOWNLOAD AT WWW.RAMONMONTAGNER.COM/RHYTHMICIMAGINATION

Filhos de Gandhi

Filhos de Gandhi

COORDINATION SYSTEMS FOR IJEXÁ

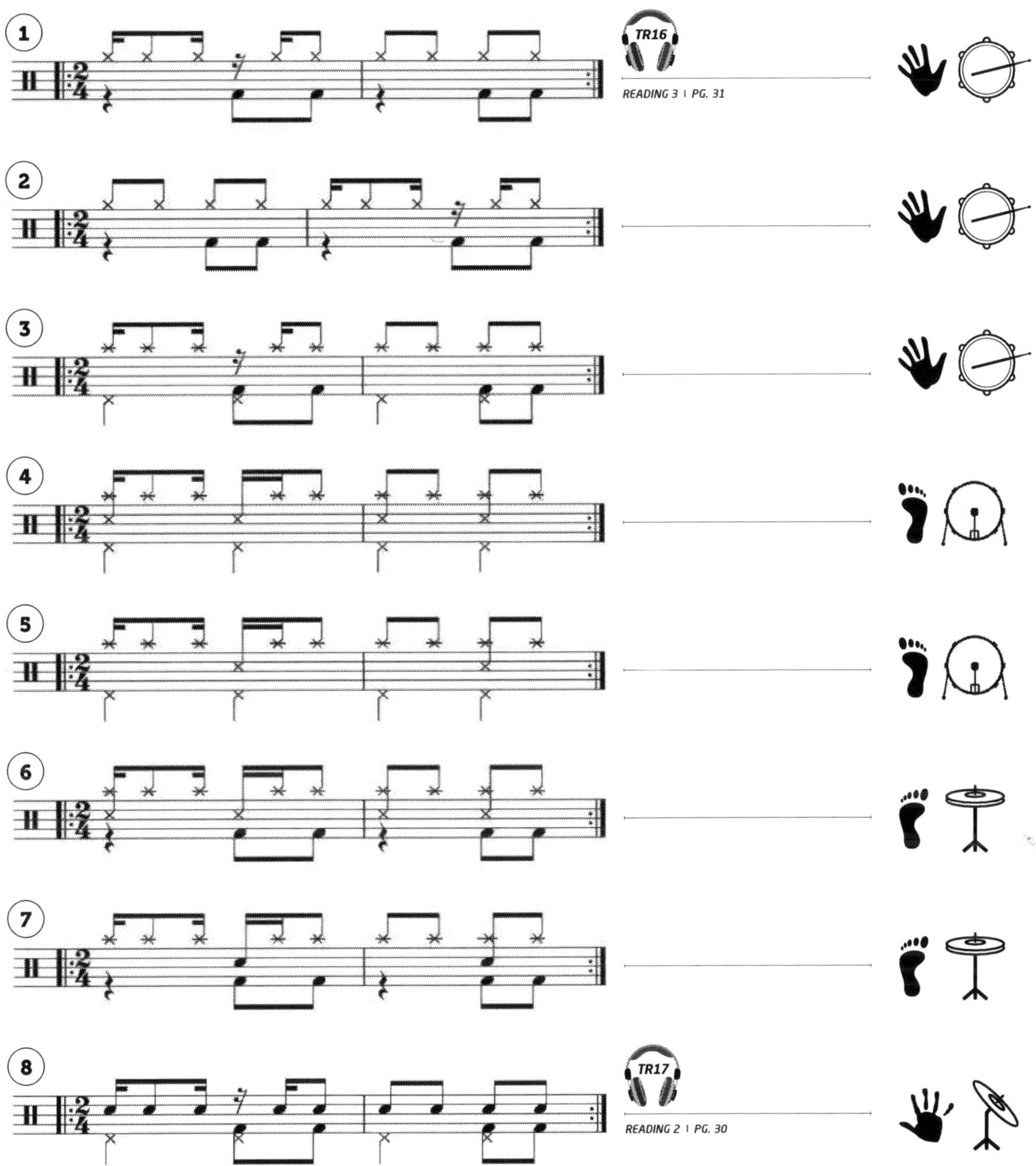

ADDITIONAL SYSTEMS

These systems require a little more patience for they are, naturally, more difficult.
Face them as though they were an appetizer for what is to come in the next units.

But stay focused!

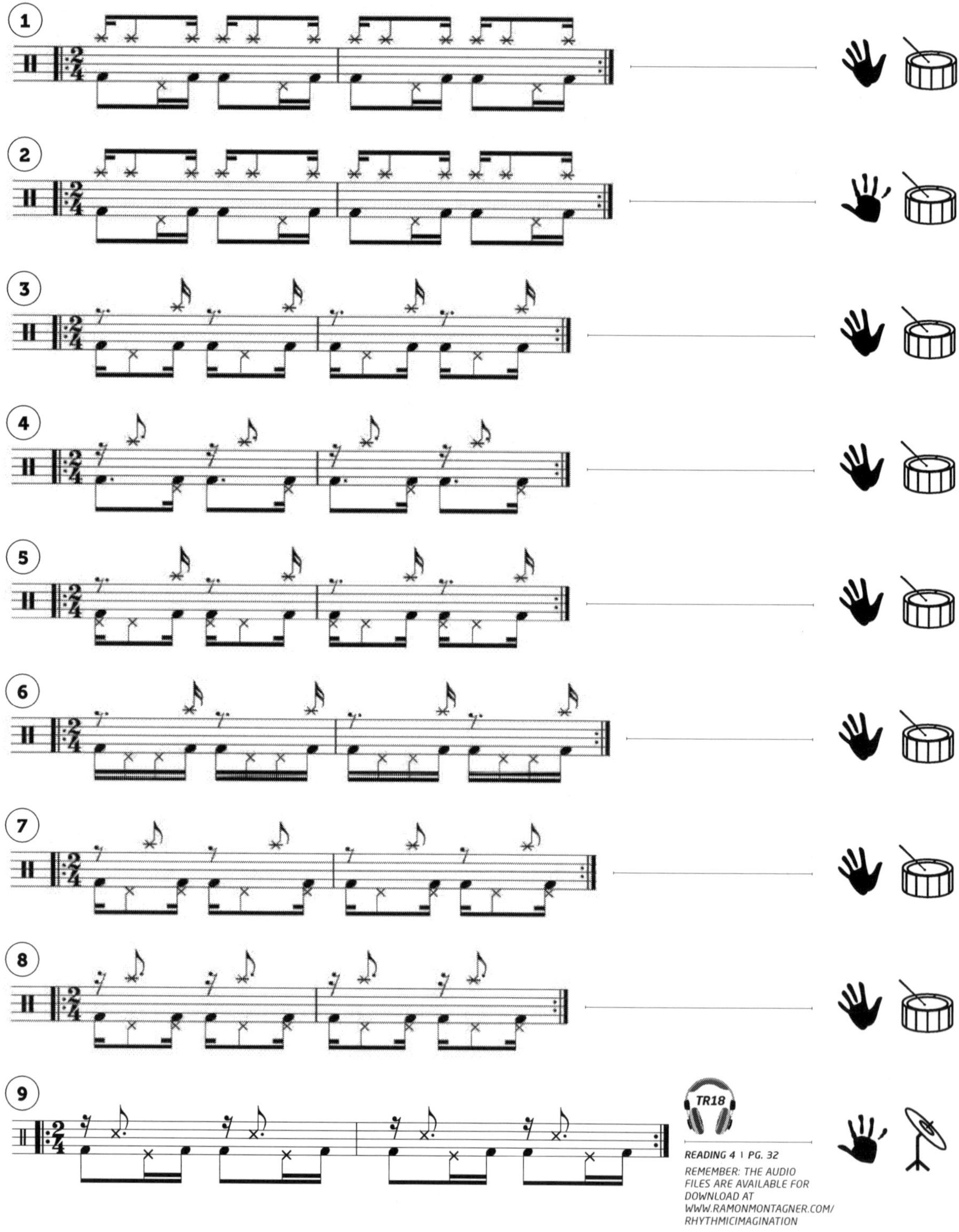

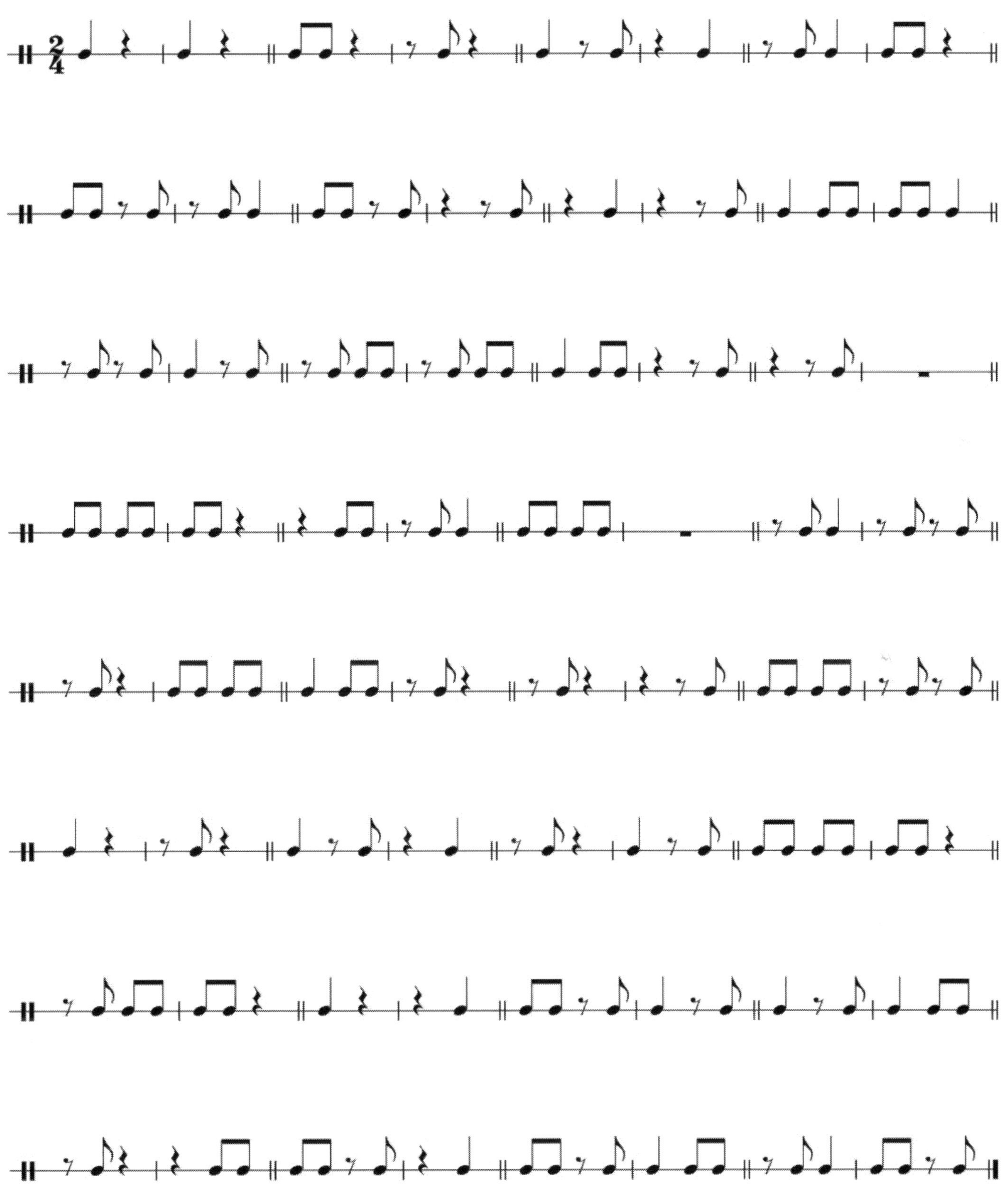

2/4

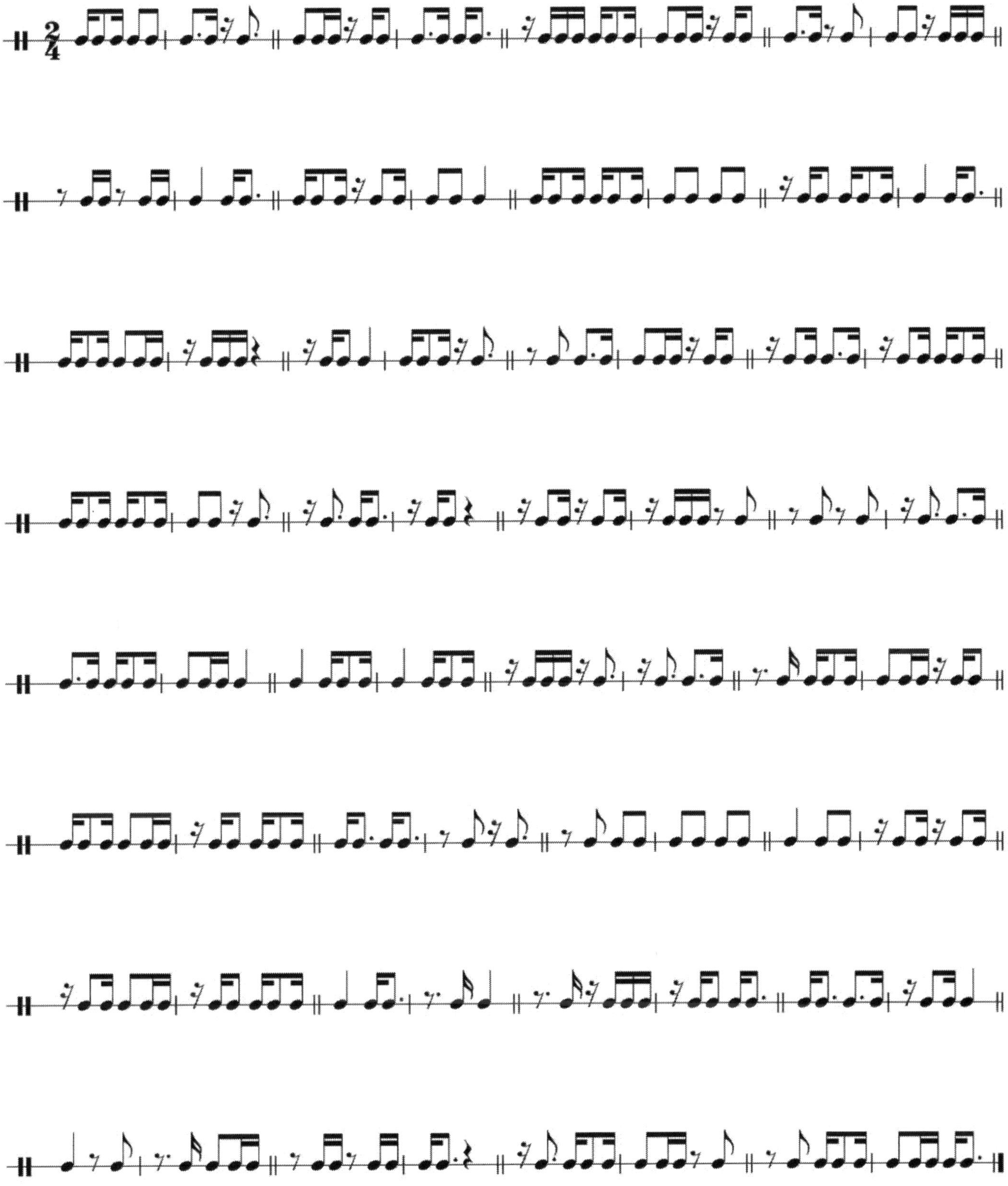

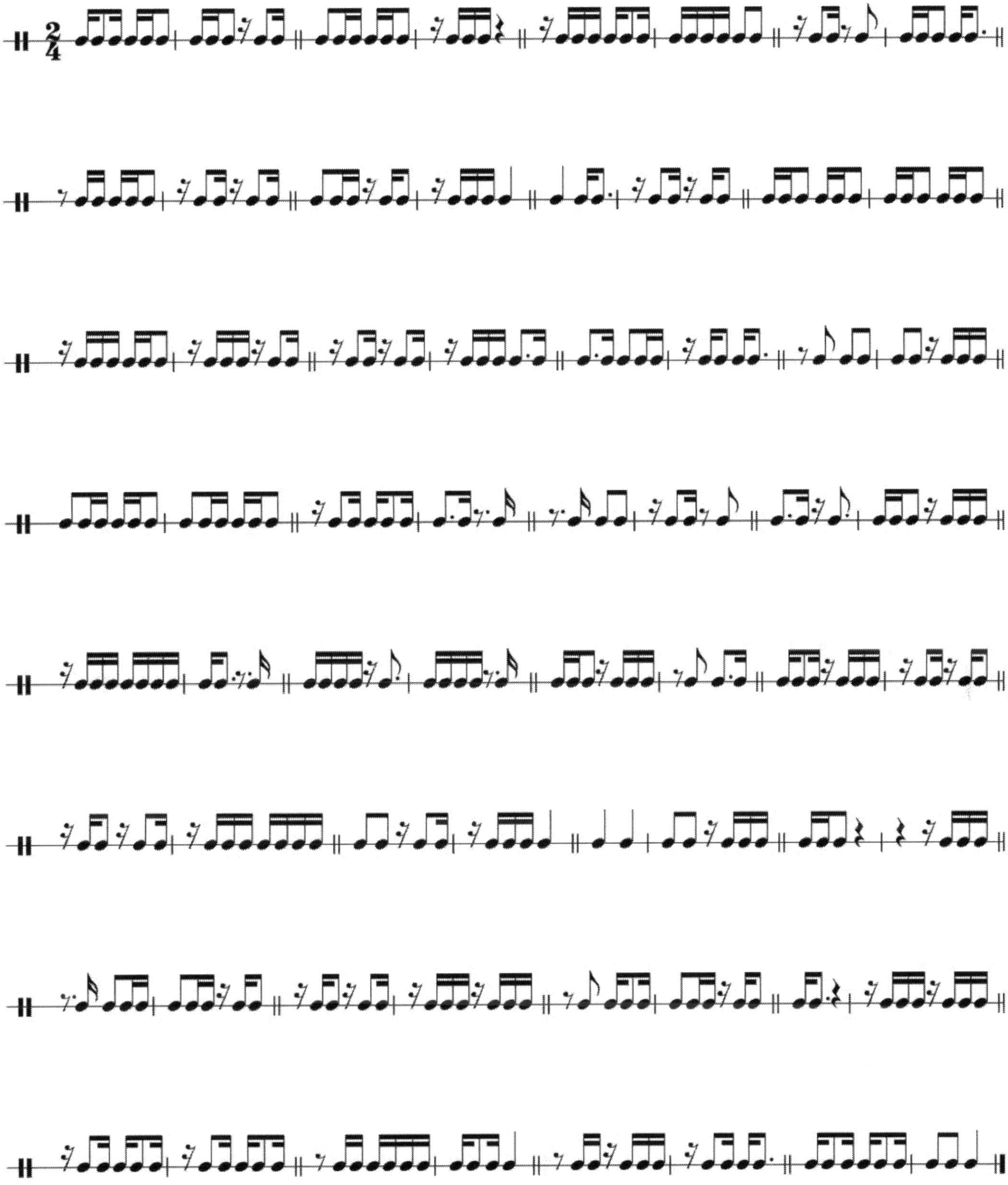

UNIT II

TWO-VOICE READING

After studying an exercise in **Norman Grossman's** book, I decided to insert here practice material for **two-voice reading**. I realized the possibilities that could be explored in terms of coordination, like reading beyond the **bass drum** and **snare**, also the **rim** and **hi-hat** on **Samba** and **Baião**, the **right** and **left hand** on **Maracatu**, and so on.

I began to work on this content at that point, and after becoming relatively fluent, this became material I recommended to my students. As I accompanied their process, the results were very interesting: greater rhythmic freedom in performance was possible.

We will begin with preparatory exercises for **two-voice reading**. Apply every exercise to all systems here proposed. **Systems 1 through 4** are directly suitable for **Samba**, and **systems 5 and 6** are recommended for **Maracatu** and **Maxixe** (another Afro-Brazilian genre strongly influenced by **Polcas** and **Lundus** which reached its peak during late 19th century and early 20th).

Systems 7 and 8 hold the characteristics of **Ijexá**. **System 9** very well suits **Baião** and its variations and, finally, **system 10** can be applied either in **Rastapé Nordestino** (Northeastern), adapted for drums in a group context, or in **Frevo** leading with the ride in a freer and personally tailored way.

> **REMEMBER TO FIND THE BEST WAY TO PRACTICE IF YOU ARE NOT RIGHT-HANDED.**

SYSTEMS FOR TWO-VOICE READING

PREPARATORY EXERCISES FOR TWO-VOICE READING

TWO-VOICE READING

2
4

UNIT III

 ## *THREE-VOICE READING*

As was done in the last chapter, I created exercises, systems and reading content for **three-voice reading**. Therefore, one line will be constant in each system, and for these I focused on the main rhythmics of Brazilian genres using them as examples. This way we will have **Samba, Baião, Ijexá** and **Maracatu** patterns.

Exercises of this kind are also be found in **Jazz** methods like *"The Studio Jazz Cookbook"* by **John Pickering**, but perhaps were never applied to Brazilian rhythms.

Before reading, there are preparatory exercises that will better enable you to read through. Naturally, variations will occur mostly on the **left hand, right** and **left foot**, leaving the **right hand** responsible for leading.

Preparatory exercises were written without defining what part is played, since that will depend on the selected systems, but the height used in the key (notation) works. For example, in **systems 1 through 6, the upper line is the left hand on snare/rim, the middle one is the right foot on bass drum, and the lower line is the left foot on hi hat**. In systems 7, 8 and 10, the **upper line will be the right hand on the ride/hi hat**, the **middle one is the left hand on snare/rim,** and the **lower one is left foot on hi hat**.

Finally, in **system 9 the upper line is right hand on ride/hi hat, middle line is right foot on bass drum and lower one is left foot on hi hat**. As was done when two-voice reading, apply each exercise to all systems proposed.

> **REMEMBER TO FIND THE BEST WAY TO PRACTICE IF YOU ARE NOT RIGHT-HANDED.**

SYSTEMS 1 THROUGH 6
- LEFT HAND ON THE SNARE / RIM
- RIGHT FOOT ON BASS DRUM
- LEFT FOOT ON HI HAT

SYSTEMS 7, 8 AND 9
- RIGHT HAND ON RIDE / HI HAT
- LEFT HAND ON SNARE / RIM
- LEFT HAND ON HI HAT

SYSTEM 10
- RIGHT HAND ON RIDE / HI HAT
- RIGHT FOOT ON BASS DRUM
- LEFT FOOT ON HI HAT

SYSTEMS FOR THREE-VOICE READING

PREPARATORY EXERCISES FOR READING THREE-VOICE READING

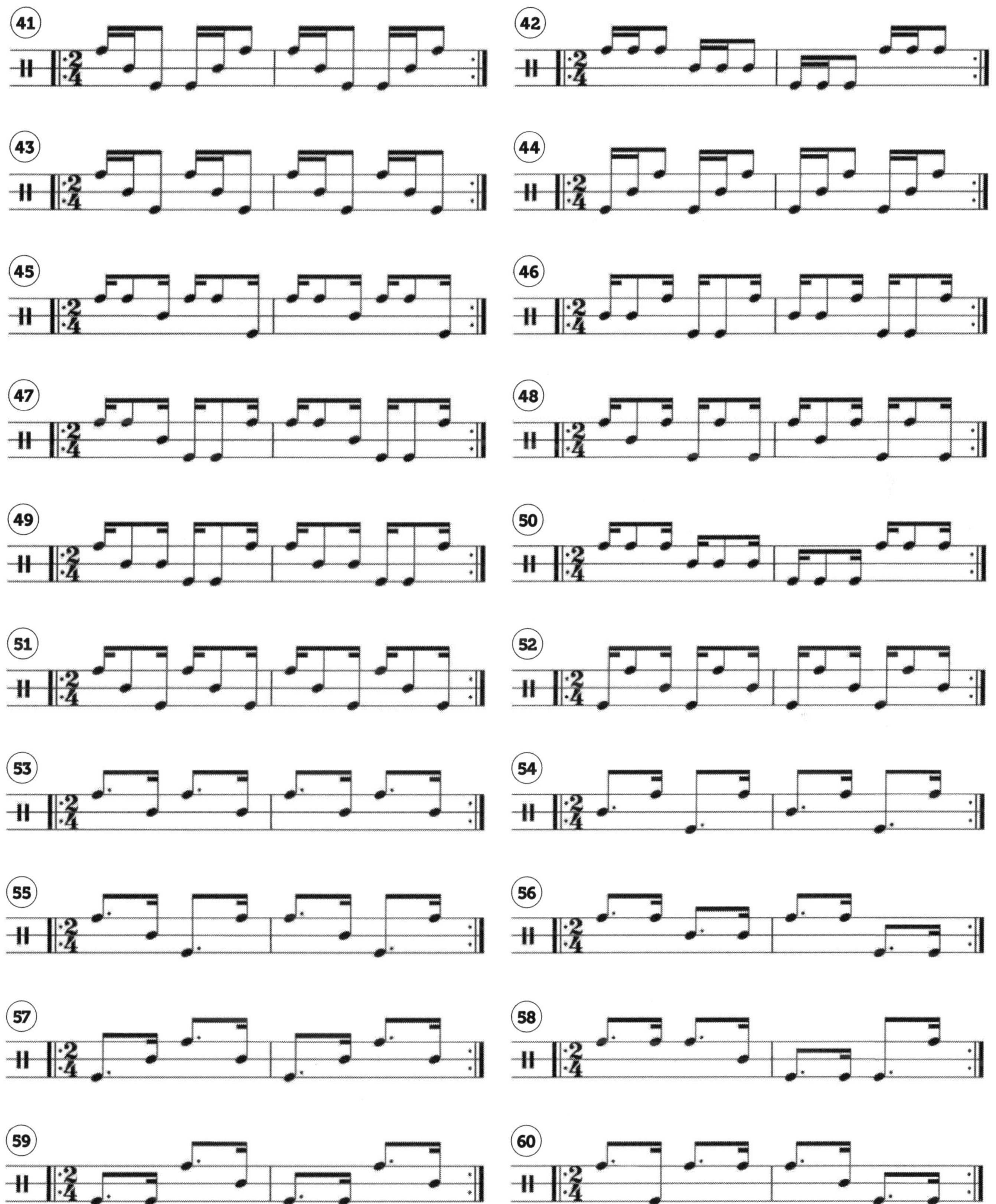

THREE-VOICE READING

2/4

UNIT IV

EXERCISES FOR HARMONIC INDEPENDENCE

What I understand by **Harmonic Independence** is the capacity to play rhythms in a freer way, executing lines with all **four-voice reading**, alternating between concepts of linearity and simultaneity, and where **two** or **more voices reading** are maintained in unison.

Brazilian rhythms are very harmonic in this sense, containing different simultaneous layers, some of which stay constant while others vary. I find that, getting to this point in the book, having practiced the other units and developed a clearer more established coordination, these studies of **Harmonic Independence** will be a natural continuation and add even more to the creativity in your playing.

I prioritized exercises for the left **hand** and **feet,** since the **right hand** has the **fundamental** role of leading when playing Brazilian rhythms.

> **REMEMBER TO FIND THE BEST WAY TO PRACTICE IF YOU ARE NOT RIGHT-HANDED.**

HARMONIC INDEPENDENCE EXERCISES

Exercises 1 through 45 should be practiced with the **right hand** leading as suggested below. Practice each exercise with all **three leading suggestions**.

And the following exercises are small solos played with more liberty. I hope they help you think in a freer way to play the leading parts.

HARMONIC INDEPENDENCE

HARMONIC INDEPENDENCE *SOLOS*

3

4

5

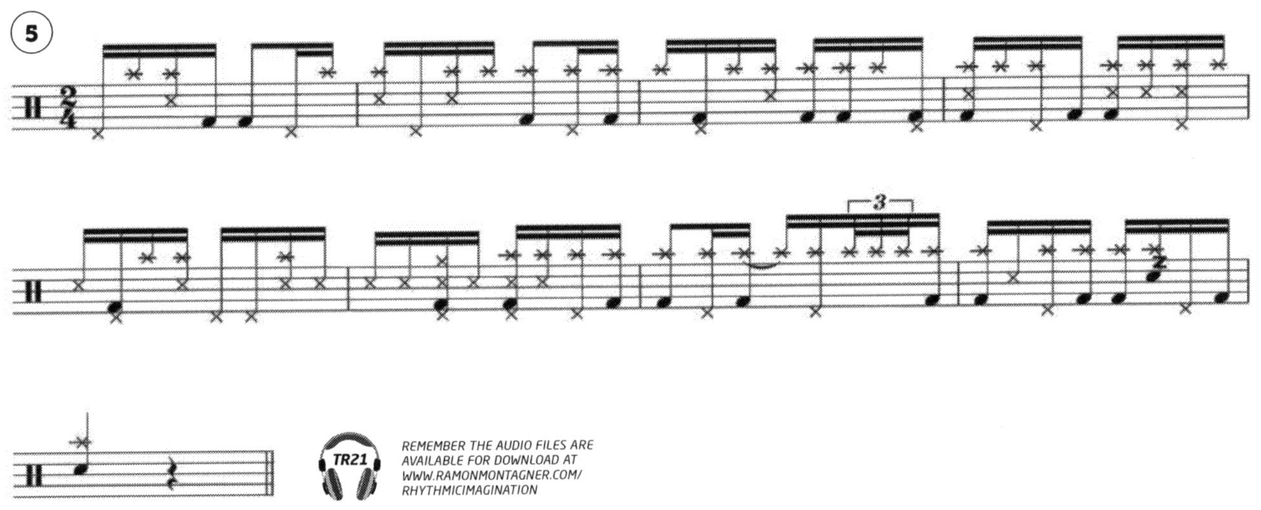

TR21
REMEMBER THE AUDIO FILES ARE
AVAILABLE FOR DOWNLOAD AT
WWW.RAMONMONTAGNER.COM/
RHYTHMICIMAGINATION

6

UNIT V

IRREGULAR TIME SIGNATURES READING IN **5/4** AND **7/8**

In this unit we will have reading and systems to play **Samba** in **5/4**, our well-known **Jequibau**, born from from Jazz influences and evolved in São Paulo in the mid-1960s.

We will also have reading and systems for **Samba** in **7/8**. I created these exercises looking to improve reading and coordination working these time signatures, since they are less usual in our day-to-day.

I chose the **Samba in 5/7** for it is more common than, for example, **Baião in 5/4** or **Ijexá in 7/8**. If you have doubts regarding the rhythms proposed, firstly resolve them with your teacher, then attempt to sing them entirely, and after that, practice them with the systems proposed.

> **REMEMBER TO FIND THE BEST WAY TO PRACTICE IF YOU ARE NOT RIGHT-HANDED.**

SYSTEMS FOR READING 5/4

READING IN 5/4

SYSTEMS FOR READING IN 7/8

ADING IN 7/8

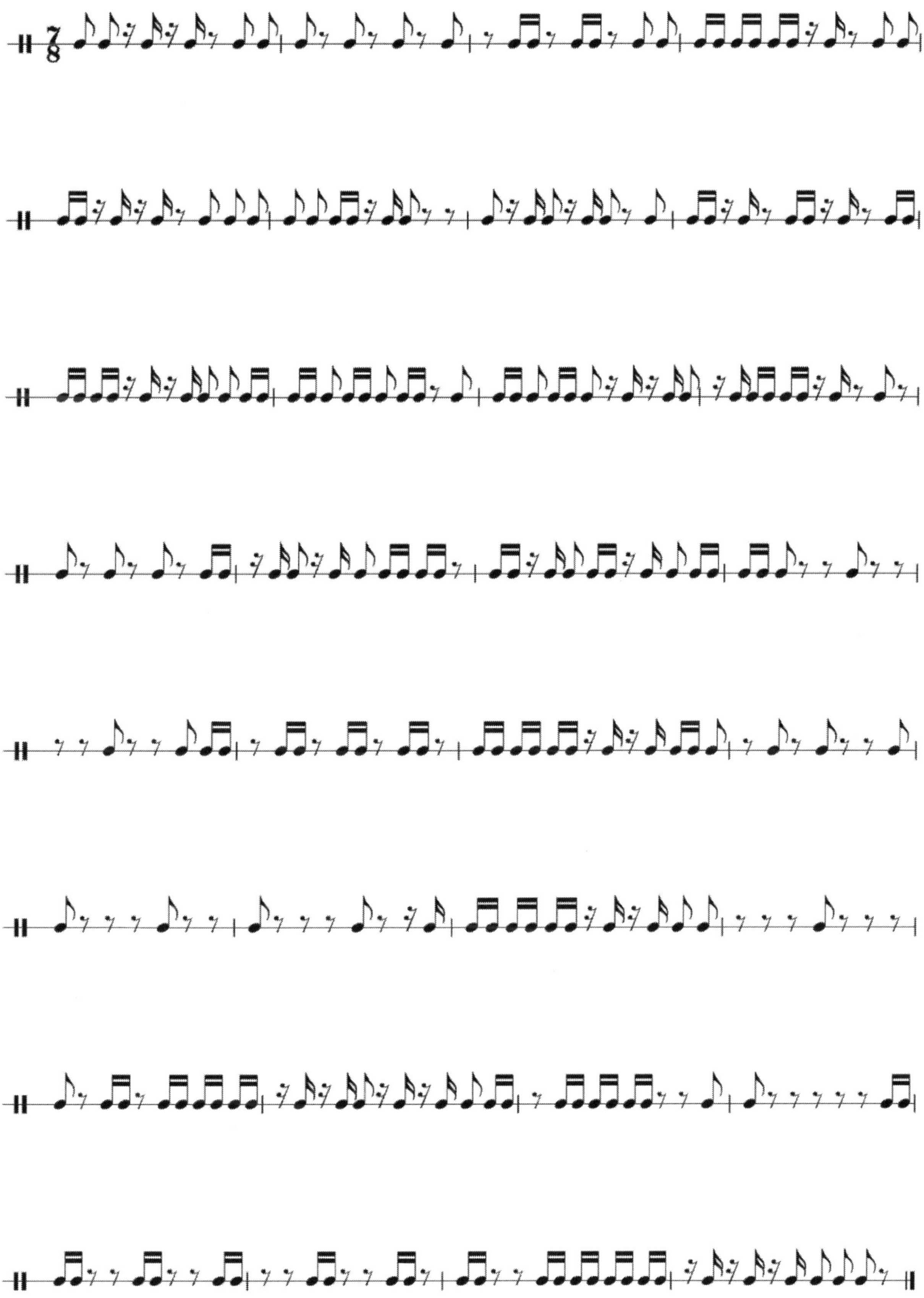

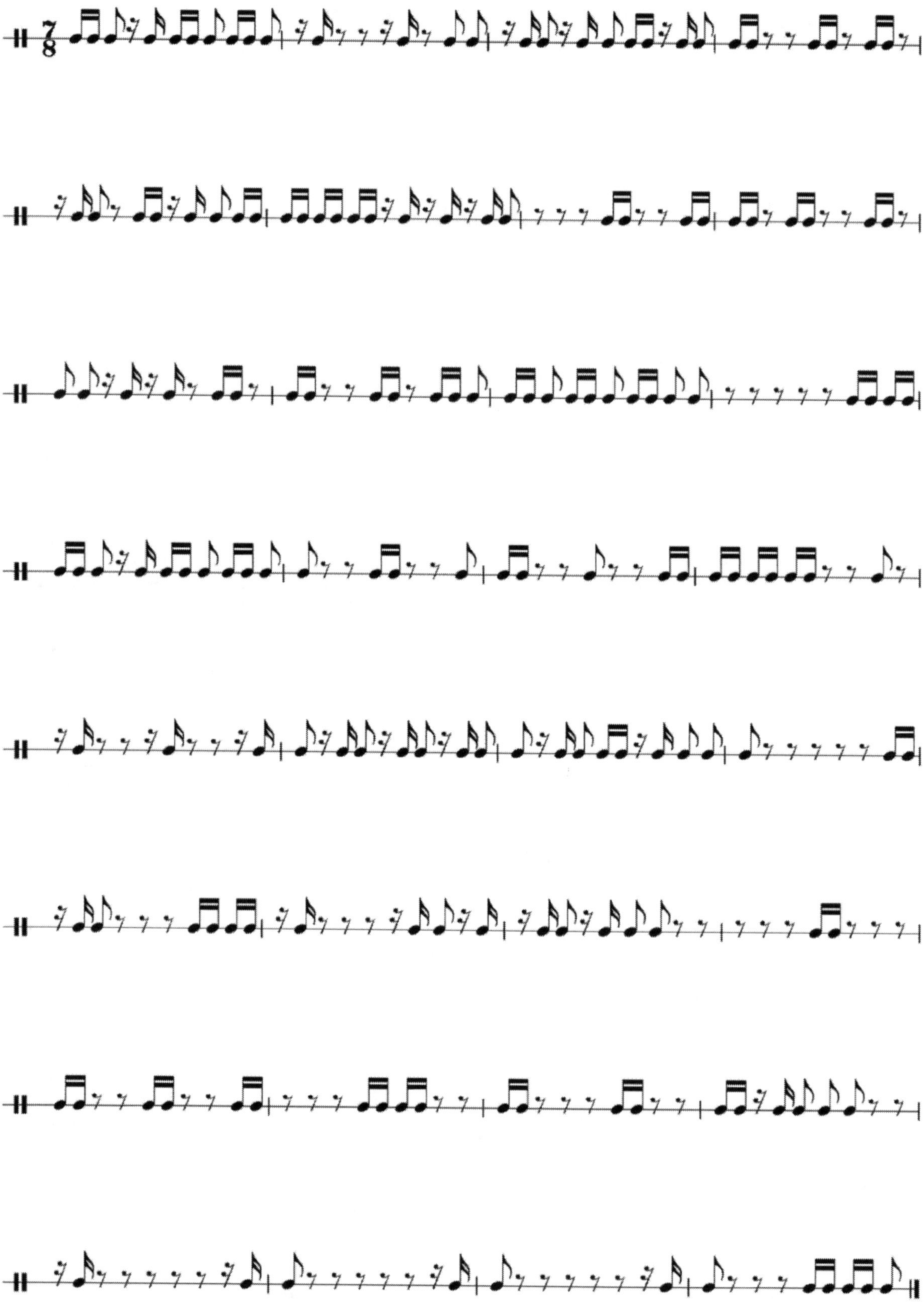

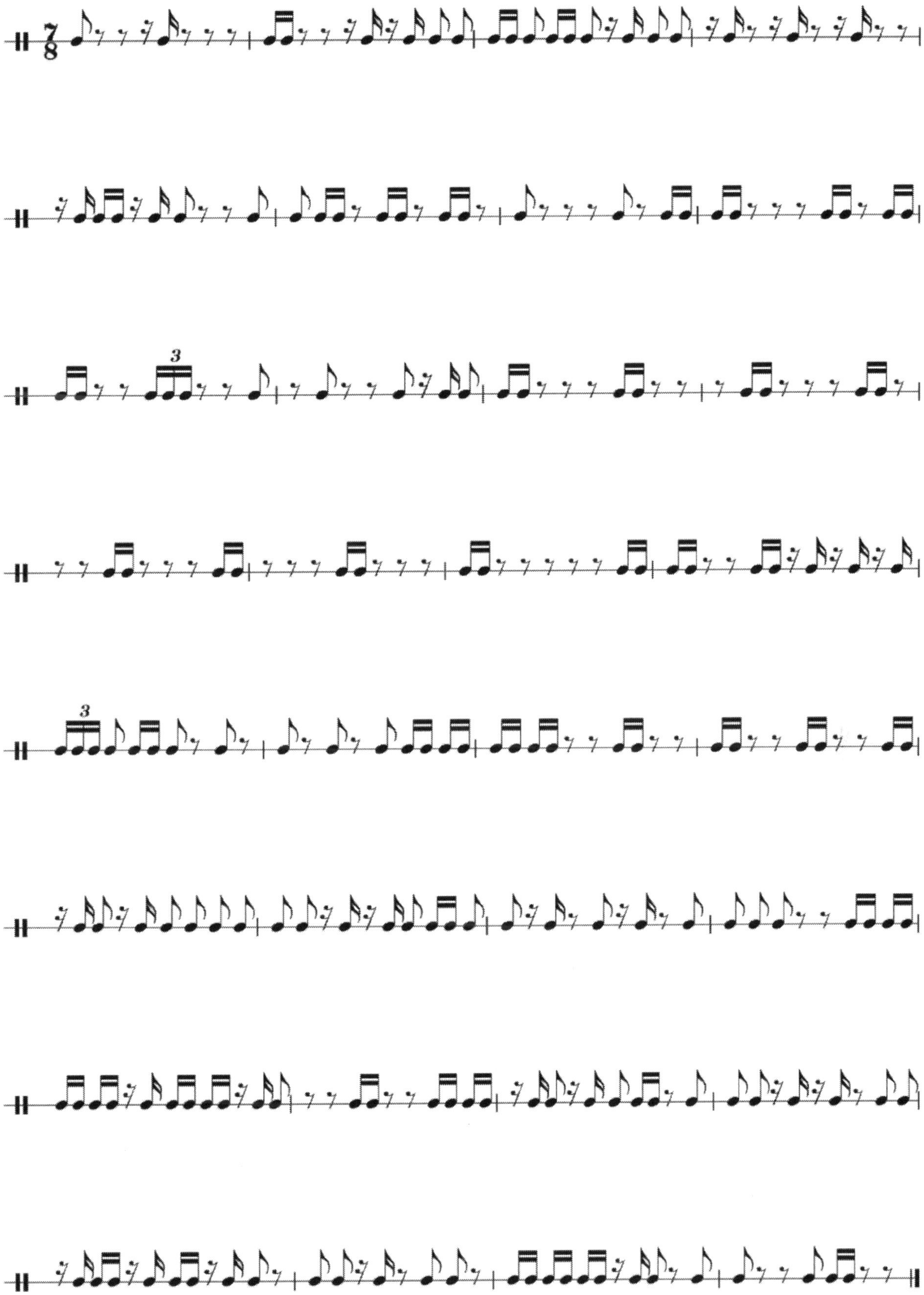

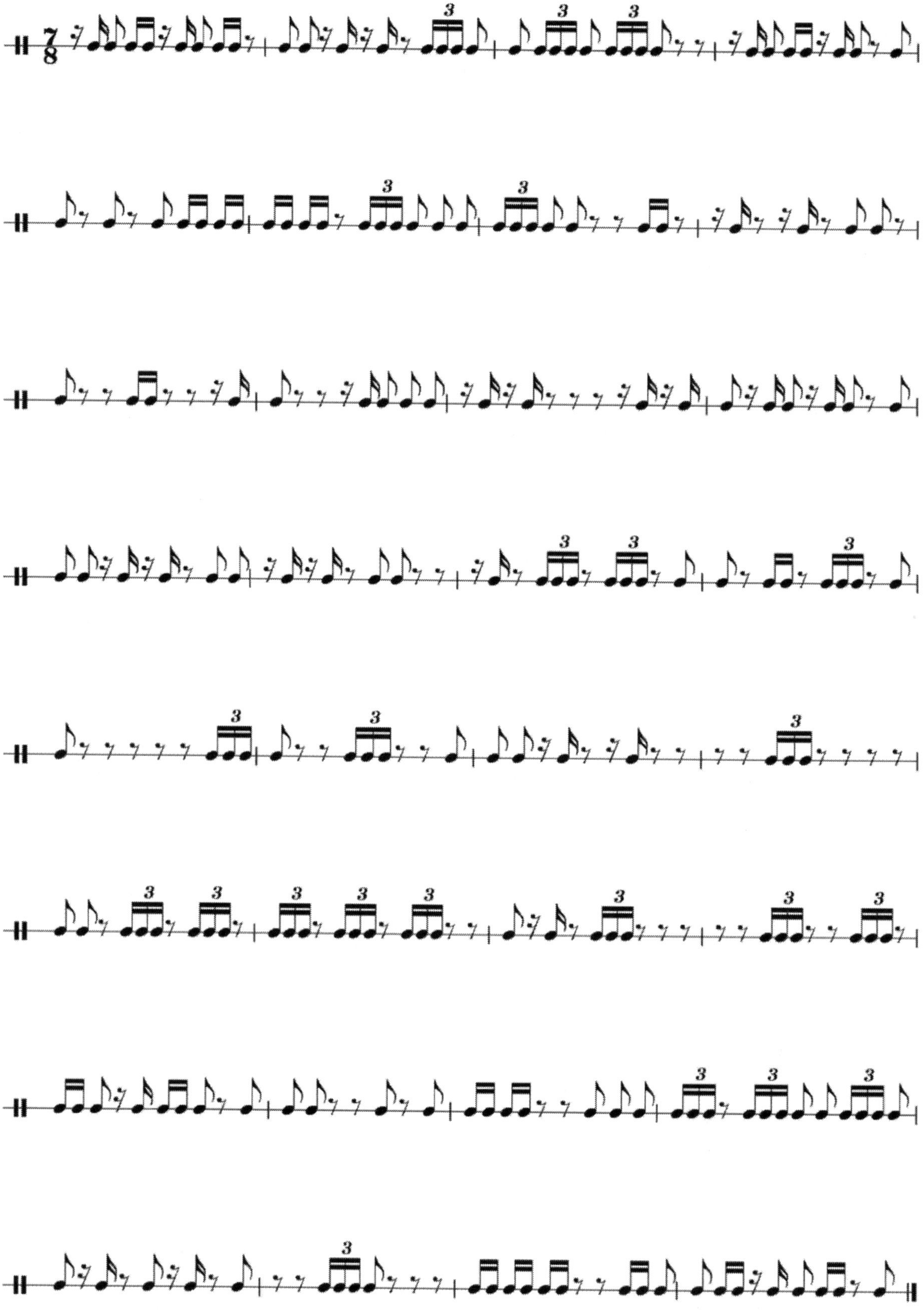

BIBLIOGRAPHY: TO PROCEED WITH YOUR PRACTICE

» *Allan Dawson* - THE COMPLETE DRUMMERS VOCABULARY AS TAUGHT BY ALLAN DAWSON | Manhattan Music Publications

» *André Tandeta* - SAMBA NA BATERIA - COORDENAÇÃO E LEITURA | Author's Edition

» *Bruno Kiefer* - HISTÓRIA DA MÚSICA BRASILEIRA - DOS PRIMÓRDIOS AO INÍCIO DO SÉCULO XX | Ed. Movimento

» *Cassio Cunha* - IPC INDEPENDÊNCIA POLIRÍTMICA COORDENADA PARA BATERIA E PERCUSSÃO | Ed. Irmãos Vitale

» *Climério de Oliveira Santos e Tarcísio Soares Resende* - MARACATU: BAQUE VIRADO E BAQUE SOLTO | Batuque Book Pernambuco

» *Christiano Rocha* - BATERIA BRASILEIRA | Author's Edition

» *Daniel Oliveira* - ESTUDOS DE POLIRRITMIA | Author's Edition

» *Gary Chester* - THE NEW BREED - SYSTEMS FOR THE DEVELOPMENT OF YOUR OWN CREATIVITY | Modern Drummer Publications, Inc

» *Gilberto de Syllos e Ramon Montagner* - BATERIA E CONTRABAIXO NA MÚSICA POPULAR BRASILEIRA | Ed. Irmãos Vitale

» *Guerra Peixe* - MARACATUS DO RECIFE | Ed. Irmãos Vitale

» *Jayme Pladevall* - BATERIA CONTEMPORÃNEA - TÉCNICA - RITMOS | Editora Vitale

» *John Pickering* - STUDIO JAZZ DRUM COOKBOOK | MelBay

» *José Ramos Tinhorão* - PEQUENA HISTÓRIA DA MÚSICA POPULAR - 1975 | Editora Vozes

» *Lauro Lellis* - O SAMBA DE CADA UM | Author's Edition

» *Lucas Van Merwijk* - ADVANCED COORDINATION STUDIES | TamTam Productions

» *Marvin Dahlgren and Eliot Fine* - 4 WAY COORDINATION | Henry Adler Inc Publication

» *Nenê* - RITMOS DO BRASIL PARA BATERIA | Author's Edition

» *Norman Grosman* - THE COMPLETE BOOK OF MODERN DRUMMING | Amsco Music Publishing Company

» *Oscar Bolão* - BATUQUE É UM PRIVILÉGIO | Ed. Lumiar

» *Peter Magadini* - POLYRHYTHMS FOR THE DRUMSET | Alfred Music Publishing

» Scott Kettner - MARACATU FOR DRUMSET AND PERCUSSION | Hal Leonard

» *Sergio Gomes* - NOVOS CAMINHOS DA BATERIA BRASILEIRA | Ed. Irmãos Vitale

» *Tito Oliveira* - RITMOS AFRO-BRASILEIROS NA BATERIA | Author's Edition

» *Vera Cruz Island* - BRAZILIAN RHYTHMS FOR DRUMSET | Hudson Music

The fantastic Ramon Montagner grants us this spectacular material. His new book "Rhythmic Imagination" is a valuable tool for our development on drums, and more specifically, in Brazilian rhythms like Samba, Baião, Maracatu, Ijexá and Frevo. The presentation of practice systems and reading is very clear and direct. The additional systems, multiple voice reading and the study of harmonic independence are sensational too. Highly recommended to the student who looks to work and improve coordination, phrasing, groove, reading, and enhancing fluency and creativity! Thank you for the present, Ramon, and let's practice, guys!

Mauricio Zottarelli   DRUMMER AND EDUCATOR

Studying Brazilian music nowadays seems easy, but when you have in your hands material like that of Ramon Montagner, you realize the difference between typical material on Brazilian music and one from someone who has dedicated his life to the understanding and to self-expression through richer musical culture in terms of rhythms from around the world. Ramon's passion is in the details, and explanations introducing Brazilian music culture are very clear throughout this book. Ramon just released a masterpiece when it comes to independence and establishes himself as one of the wisest in the topic in Brazil, and in the world! Thank you so much for your dedication and for the gift that is this fantastic material.

Aquiles Priester   DRUMMER AND EDUCATOR

Rhythmic Imagination is a book that already starts out differently, audacious from the cover and the layout. This material demonstrates the serious research done over years and the carefully planned characteristic idioms of one of the great representatives of modern Brazilian drumming: Ramon Montagner. Now Ramon makes available this precious material in a asystematized way, which is sure to help drummers discover new possibilities in performing with the instrument in an advanced level of coordination inside the language of Brazilian drumming. Thank you, Ramon, for showing us new paths to be explored in our journey with the drums! As Ramon himself says, rephrasing the great Portuguese poet Fernando Pessoa: "Drumming is precise!!!" So let's dive into our rhythmic imagination!

Giba Favery   MUSICIAN, EDUCATOR AND AUTHOR

Indispensable book for any drummer that seeks to dig deeper into independence and to know a different approach to Brazilian rhythms. Congratulations, Ramon!

Carlos Bala   DRUMMER

Ramon did an exquisite job with his book "Rhythmic Imagination". It is surely one of the most in-depth books on coordination and independence on drums that I have seen on Brazilian rhythms. I recommend it to everyone! Thank you, Ramon, for such a gift that is this source of practice for an entire generation.

Christiano Galvão   DRUMMER AND AUTHOR

Congratulations for sharing this new method, the result of a lot of dedication to the instrument, which makes your technique and musicality something seem easy. Easy it is to comment on a great musician!

Celso de Almeida   DRUMMER AND EDUCATOR

There is nothing like practicing Brazilian drums through the real adaptations of percussion lines. It is real, authentic, and, of course,at the maximum level of coordination!

Daniel Oliveira   DRUMMER AND EDUCATOR

When I walk by his practice room (which is right next to mine, to my despair), sometimes it seems like there are three guys playing in there. But it's "just" him, playing alone. That being said, there is nothing better than a book focused on coordination written by a nut like him. Actually, it's not only about coordination, for "Rhythmic Imagination – Brazilian Rhythms Coordination Studies" will further help the student to improve their rhythmic reading, as well as to acquire liberty to play Brazilian music at a high level.
Congratulations for this beautiful work, my dear friend. May this take on the world! And thank you for making me lose sleep with this book!

Christiano Rocha   MUSICIAN, EDUCATOR E AUTHOR

This book will twist your brain completely. It will help you understand a little more of the sensational rhythmic complexity of Ramon's playing, and take your drumming performance to the next level.

Vlad Rocha   DRUMMER AND EDUCATOR

"Brazilian Rhythms Coordination Studies" is a practical and functional book, but also very challenging. With it, the drummer learns to control all four limbs, working hands and feet combining reading on Samba, Baião, Maracatu, Ijexã and much more. As Ramon himself mentions in the book, "Our journey requires time and determination. Shall we?" And I accept the challenge... Let's! Congratulations, Ramon. Much success to you!

Vera Figueiredo DRUMMER AND EDUCATOR

Some musicians impress with their musical breadth and the ease by which they absorb and incorporate music, whether it is classical or modern, and with notable creativity and good taste they establish new paradigms. Ramon Montagner fits perfectly into these attributes, and hearing him play gives us the conviction that the drums are going through full and complex musical evolution.

Jayme Pladevall DRUMMER AND EDUCATOR

ACKNOWLEDGEMENTS

I thank **Jesus Christ** for everything in my life; to my wife **Lidia** and my children **Lorena** and **Matheus** for their patience and love; to my brother **Rodrigo Montagner** for the proofreading; to **Vlad** for the efforts in sheetmusic and precious opinions; to **Mauricio Geurgas** from Gráfica Exacta, friend and student, for the layout; to the dear friends **Rayne Moraes, Fabio Meneguin Marques** and **Marcelo Lima** for always being together helping so much; to the masters **Brasa, Jayme Pladevall** and **Lilian Carmona** for the teachings and the friendship; to the great **Augusto Silva** for *Frevo* consulting; to the dear super-drummers **Carlos Bala, Celso de Almeida, Edu Ribeiro, Christiano Rocha, Lilian Carmona, Vera Figueiredo, Phil Maturano, Casey Scheuerell, Daniel Bédard, Mark Eeftens, Lucas van Merwijk, Mauricio Zottarelli, Christiano Galvão, John Riley, Giba Favery, Aquiles Priester,** for opinions and suggestions; and to the dear **Daniel Oliveira**, for the friendship and encouragement.